Building a Joint Cyber Weapons Acquisition Program in the Marine Corps

Software Acquisition Pathway Lessons Learned

MEGAN MCKERNAN, RYAN CONSAUL, BRADLEY WILSON,
JOHN YURCHAK, COLIN D. SMITH, MICHAEL J. D. VERMEER,
GEOFFREY MCGOVERN, THOMAS GOUGHNOUR,
DEVIN TIERNEY, HANSELL PEREZ

Prepared for the United States Marine Corps
Approved for public release; distribution is unlimited

 NATIONAL DEFENSE RESEARCH INSTITUTE

For more information on this publication, visit **www.rand.org/t/RRA1888-1**.

About RAND

The RAND Corporation is a research organization that develops solutions to public policy challenges to help make communities throughout the world safer and more secure, healthier and more prosperous. RAND is nonprofit, nonpartisan, and committed to the public interest. To learn more about RAND, visit www.rand.org.

Research Integrity

Our mission to help improve policy and decisionmaking through research and analysis is enabled through our core values of quality and objectivity and our unwavering commitment to the highest level of integrity and ethical behavior. To help ensure our research and analysis are rigorous, objective, and nonpartisan, we subject our research publications to a robust and exacting quality-assurance process; avoid both the appearance and reality of financial and other conflicts of interest through staff training, project screening, and a policy of mandatory disclosure; and pursue transparency in our research engagements through our commitment to the open publication of our research findings and recommendations, disclosure of the source of funding of published research, and policies to ensure intellectual independence. For more information, visit www.rand.org/about/principles.

RAND's publications do not necessarily reflect the opinions of its research clients and sponsors.

About This Report

U.S. Marine Corps Systems Command's (MARCORSYSCOM's) Joint Cyber Weapons (JCW) acquisition program provides advanced cyberwarfare capabilities to support U.S. Marine Corps Forces Cyberspace Command, U.S. Cyber Command, combatant commanders, and other federal government agencies' global operations. MARCORSYSCOM requested that the RAND Corporation assist in documenting JCW program acquisition plans. Specifically, RAND researchers were asked to assist the JCW program office in refining key acquisition artifacts required for submission during the planning phase of the Software Acquisition Pathway (SWP) within the U.S. Department of Defense's (DoDs) Adaptive Acquisition Framework.[1] The research results were integrated into the program's Acquisition Strategy, Cybersecurity Strategy, Intellectual Property Strategy, Information Support Plan, Lifecycle Cost Estimate, Product Support Strategy, Test Strategy, and User Agreement. This satisfied a condition for the program to enter the execution phase of the SWP to provide rapid cyber operations capabilities to the warfighter.

In this report, we present the lessons learned and observations from this effort to help inform future JCW program acquisition information requirements and educate other DoD SWP program planning efforts.

The research reported here was completed in May 2023 and underwent security review with the sponsor before public release.

RAND National Security Research Division

This research was sponsored by MARCORSYSCOM and conducted within the Navy and Marine Forces Program of the RAND National Security Research Division (NSRD), which operates the National Defense Research Institute (NDRI), a federally funded research and development center sponsored by the Office of the Secretary of Defense, the Joint Staff, the Unified

---

[1] Defense Acquisition University (DAU) applies the term *artifacts* to the set of documentation deliverables required for each pathway.

Combatant Commands, the Navy, the Marine Corps, the defense agencies, and the defense intelligence enterprise.

For more information on the RAND Navy and Marine Forces Program, see www.rand.org/nsrd/nmf or contact the director (contact information is provided on the webpage).

Acknowledgments

We thank David Pasquill, Product Manager, Program Management Office, Marine Corps Cyberspace Operations, for his guidance and insight during the development of the SWP documents described in this report. We also thank Col Thomas Dono, Maj Matthew Gurrister, Torrence Moore, Vincent Monroe, Jermaine Kendall, and Nichole Sillaman, who provided valuable support to this effort.

We also thank Timothy Conley and Chad Heitzenrater for their constructive and thorough reviews of this analysis. Finally, Paul DeLuca and Brendan Toland, Director and Associate Director, respectively, of the Navy and Marine Forces Program, provided valuable guidance and insightful comments on the research.

Summary

Issue

U.S. Marine Corps Systems Command's (MARCORSYSCOM's) Joint Cyber Weapons (JCW) acquisition program provides advanced cyberwarfare capabilities to support Marine Corps Forces Cyberspace Command, U.S. Cyber Command, combatant commanders, and other federal government agencies' global operations. The cyber operational environment is unpredictable, and the windows in which the Marine Corps might leverage vulnerabilities to create cyber weapons can be short and uncertain.[2] This dynamic necessitates that the acquisition and operational communities that are involved in acquiring or developing the cyber weapons have the flexibility to adapt to the rapidly changing environment. Because of this challenge, MARCORSYSCOM is making use of U.S. Department of Defense's (DoD's) Software Acquisition Pathway (SWP) to enable the most appropriate and expeditious path possible when acquiring and fielding cyber weapons.[3] However, official policy guidance on the SWP was released as recently as October 2020; the Marine Corps had very few other initiatives making use of the guidance, and none of those initiatives were as unique as offensive cyber weapons. MARCORSYSCOM asked RAND researchers to help assess, tailor, and develop the program strategy taking these uncertainties into consideration.

---

[2] Bradley Wilson, Thomas Goughnour, Megan McKernan, Andrew Karode, Devin Tierney, Mark V. Arena, Michael J. D. Vermeer, Hansell Perez, and Alexis Levedahl, *A Cost Estimating Framework for U.S. Marine Corps Joint Cyber Weapons*, RAND Corporation, RR-A1124-1, 2023.

[3] *SWP* is the commonly used abbreviation for DoD's Software Acquisition Pathway throughout DAU's Adaptive Acquisition Framework (AAF) internet portal postings and in the Undersecretary of Defense for Acquisition and Sustainment office's published documentation on AAF.

Approach

With this research, we build on prior RAND research from fiscal year 2021 that brought together data on operational capability, scheduling, and uncertainty to develop a life-cycle cost-estimating framework for the JCW program.[4] The program strategies that RAND researchers assisted with were the Acquisition Strategy, Cybersecurity Strategy, Intellectual Property Strategy, Information Support Plan, Lifecycle Cost Estimate, Product Support Strategy, Test Strategy, and User Agreement.

Completing these acquisition artifacts required a multipronged methodology.[5] Tasks consisted of a review of relevant SWP statutes, regulations, and policy, along with other program documentation prepared for such purposes as market research or budget justifications; discussions with key stakeholders in the requirements, acquisition, and user communities; and the development of a detailed schedule to track important deadlines and coordination points.

Key Insights and Recommendations

The artifacts we developed were needed to satisfy a condition for the JCW program to enter the execution phase of the SWP to provide rapid cyber operations capabilities to the warfighter.

From our experiences assisting with the SWP artifacts for the JCW program, we were able to glean some lessons learned that might be beneficial for other programs. Our analysis identified the following key insights:

- Prioritizing the acquisition artifact development schedule is necessary to meet planning phase timelines because some artifacts depend on content required in others.

---

[4] Wilson et al., 2023.

[5] DAU's AAF internet portal applies the term *artifacts* to the set of documentation deliverables that programs are required to develop on the pathway. The AAF Document Identification tool on DAU's AAF portal provides guidance on which statutory requirements and documentary artifacts are required for each pathway. The AAF Document Identification tool also assists in tailoring AAF program documentation.

- The preplanning phase did not provide much useful information that is needed to scope the SWP artifacts.
- Early and ongoing coordination between stakeholders is beneficial for the program.
- Tailoring is a key element in drafting relevant artifacts in the SWP.
- Leveraging the User Agreement is a useful way to define stakeholder roles and relationships in a software development process that aligns with agile principles and stakeholder's approval needs.
- Current SWP policy and strategy templates are not designed with offensive cyber software in mind.
- The JCW's artifact sign-off approach was expeditious; stakeholders typically signed off within a few months. This could indicate that SWP provides useful flexibility to programs.

The JCW Product Manager and Lead User Representative closely coordinated to provide Decision Authorities (DAs) with adequate and timely information to inform decisionmaking. Furthermore, the JCW program office tailored documentation, such as the Information Support Plan, to meet its needs but only after deliberations and consultation with program and MARCORSYSCOM leadership.

Using the above insights, we provide the following recommendations to better position SWP programs for success in the planning phase:

- Programs can take several actions to prioritize planning task schedules, such as dedicating staff (including contract support) to concentrating on planning phase documentation, prebriefing signatories prior to document delivery, and early development of classification guidance.
- Programs should establish coordination mechanisms before and during the planning phase in order to work seamlessly between stakeholders during the planning phase. This coordination will help mitigate potential risks to the schedule and minimize the impact of the risks that might emerge.

- Programs should tailor SWP documentation to their needs.[6] However, effective tailoring should be a conscious upfront decision and require leadership support and critical thinking on what is applicable to the program.
- Programs should establish an adaptive and continuous requirements management process within the User Agreement for the management and translation of high-level capability needs into functional requirements, software development goals, and testing targets.
- The Office of the Secretary of Defense should consider developing modified guidance and reporting metrics for cyber weapon SWP programs because they are significantly different forms of software compared with typical continuously operated systems.

---

[6] Appendix J of Department of Defense Standard Practice MIL-STD-881F could be useful for providing a framework for tailoring acquisition documentation based on the work breakdown structure of their programs (Department of Defense Standard Practice MIL-STD-881F, *Work Breakdown Structures for Defense Material Items*, U.S. Department of Defense, May 13, 2022).

Contents

Figures and Tables

Figures

Tables

CHAPTER 1

Introduction

Because of the long timelines and significant cost traditionally associated with acquiring weapon systems for the U.S. Department of Defense (DoD), analyses are constantly being conducted to find ways to streamline acquisition and reduce cost. In the past five years, the Advisory Panel on Streamlining and Codifying Acquisition Regulations (Section 809 Panel), the Defense Innovation Board (DIB), and the Defense Science Board (DSB) each published a series of findings on acquisition reform and software acquisition in particular.[1] Taking into account findings from various analyses on acquisition along with direction from Congress,[2] in January 2020, DoD released an instruction defining the Adaptive Acquisition Framework (AAF) to

---

[1] For example, see Defense Technical Information Center, "Section 809 Panel," webpage, undated; DIB, *Software Is Never Done: Refactoring the Acquisition Code for Competitive Advantage*, U.S. Department of Defense, May 3, 2019b; DSB, *Design and Acquisition of Software for Defense Systems*, U.S. Department of Defense, February 2018. Note that Congress created the Section 809 Panel in the fiscal year (FY) 2016 National Defense Authorization Act (NDAA) (Public Law 114-92, National Defense Authorization Act for Fiscal Year 2016, November 25, 2015). From 2016 to 2019, the panel released five publications, which included 98 recommendations for change in the defense acquisition system. Section 872 of the FY18 NDAA required the DIB to examine how to streamline software development and acquisition (Public Law 115–91, National Defense Authorization Act for Fiscal Year 2018, December 12, 2017). The DIB submitted its final report to Congress in May 2019. The report included ten primary recommendations and 16 additional recommendations to address hurdles in modernizing DoD's software acquisitions.

[2] Public Law 116-92, National Defense Authorization Act for Fiscal Year 2020, December 20, 2019.

improve the timeliness and affordability of acquisition programs.[3] The AAF provides six "acquisition pathways," as shown in Figure 1.1, each of which offers a life-cycle framework tailored to the characteristics of different types of acquisition programs.[4] One of these pathways, Major Capability Acquisition, preserves the traditional management framework and life cycle associated with major systems programs that is documented in the previous version of DoDI 5000.02.

The Software Acquisition Pathway (SWP) is one of the six acquisition pathways established by the AAF. According to DoD policy, the purpose of the SWP is "to facilitate rapid and iterative delivery of software capability (e.g., software-intensive systems or software-intensive components or subsystems) to the user."[5] The SWP "values working software over comprehensive documentation."[6]

One of the focuses of the SWP is the use of modern software development practices (e.g., Development, Security, and Operations [DevSecOps]). Within the SWP, programs may use either the embedded software path (for software embedded in weapon systems or other military hardware) or the application path (for software on commercial hardware or cloud platforms).[7] The SWP has a planning phase and execution phase, each of which have active user engagement.[8] The planning phase is the time during which most of the acquisition artifacts are initially developed. Programs then design,

---

[3] Department of Defense Instruction (DoDI) 5000.02, *Operation of the Adaptive Acquisition Framework*, U.S. Department of Defense, January 23, 2020, p. 4.

[4] DoDI 5000.02, 2020, p. 10.

[5] DoDI 5000.02, 2020, p. 14.

[6] Defense Acquisition University (DAU), "Develop Strategies," webpage, undated-f.

[7] Sean Brady, "DoD's Software Acquisition Pathway: Digital Delivery at the Speed of Relevance, First Annual State of the SWP," Let's Talk Agile Series briefing, October 6, 2021, p. 30. Additionally, a new pathway within the SWP for defense business systems is being planned. Public Law 116-283, William M. (Mac) Thornberry National Defense Authorization Act for Fiscal Year 2021, November 27, 2019, Section 835.

[8] Sean Brady, "DoD's Software Acquisition Pathway, Digital Delivery at the Speed of Relevance, DAU West" Let's Talk Agile briefing, January 6, 2020; DAU, "Software Acquisition," webpage, undated-k.

FIGURE 1.1

Adaptive Acquisition Framework Pathways

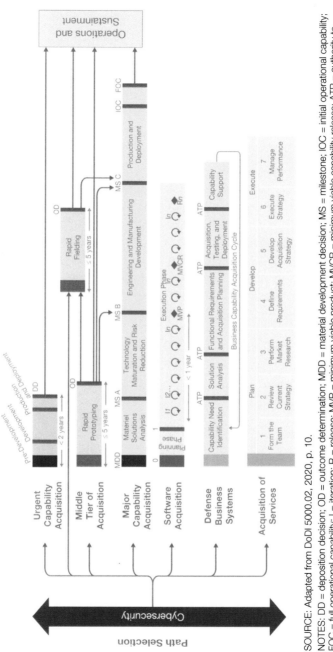

SOURCE: Adapted from DoDI 5000.02, 2020, p. 10.

NOTES: DD = deposition decision; MDD = material development decision; MS = milestone; IOC = initial operational capability; FOC = full operational capability; OD = outcome determination; I = iteration; R = release; MVP = minimum viable product; MVCR = minimum viable capability release; ATP = authority to proceed.

deliver, and operate software capabilities during the execution phase.[9] The SWP is illustrated in Figure 1.2.

Software Acquisition Policy

The U.S. Congress has been interested in DoD's software modernization and how to accelerate it for many years. For example, in the NDAAs from FY18 to FY22, there were 18 sections directly related to this topic, as shown in Table 1.1.

Over the past few decades, software modernization has been happening at a rapid pace, with many changes in industry best practices and lessons learned in software development practices.[10] A challenge for DoD has been understanding if, when, and how to adapt those lessons to government software acquisition.

DoDI 5000.87 is in place specifically to guide program offices, functional acquisition experts, and decisionmakers through DoD's software acquisition.[11] The instruction provides key information on SWP programs. These programs

- are not subject to the Joint Capabilities Integration and Development System (JCIDS) process and are not treated as major defense acquisition programs

FIGURE 1.2
Software Acquisition Pathway

SOURCE: Adapted from DoDI 5000.02, 2020, p. 10.

---

[9] DoDI 5000.87, *Operation of the Software Acquisition Pathway*, U.S. Department of Defense, October 2, 2020.

[10] For example, Gartner, a consulting firm, has documented research and surveys for more than a decade on the evolution of agile software practices and actively maintains a compilation of reviews and ratings for enterprise agile planning and management tools on its Peer Insights internet portal (Gartner Peer Insights, homepage, undated).

[11] DoDI 5000.87, 2020.

TABLE 1.1

Congressional Provisions on Department of Defense Software Modernization in National Defense Authorization Acts (FY 2018– 2022)

FY for NDAA	NDAA Provision
FY22	Section 835: Independent Study on Technical Debt in Software-Intensive Systems
FY22	Section 836: Cadre of Software Development and Acquisition Experts
FY22	Section 1522: Legacy Information Technologies and Systems Accountability
FY22	Section 1531: Digital Development Infrastructure Plan and Working Group
FY21	Section 812: Inclusion of Software in Government Performance of Acquisition Functions
FY21	Section 834: Pilot Program on the Use of Consumption-Based Solutions to Address Software-Intensive Warfighting Capability
FY21	Section 835: Balancing Security and Innovation in Software Development and Acquisition
FY21	Section 838: Comptroller General Report on Implementation of Software Acquisition Reforms
FY20	Section 230: Policy on the Talent Management of Digital Expertise and Software Professionals
FY20	Section 231: Digital Engineering Capability to Automate Testing and Evaluation
FY20	Section 255: Department-Wide Software Science and Technology Strategy.
FY20	Section 800: Authority for Continuous Integration and Delivery of Software Applications and Upgrades to Embedded Systems
FY19	Section 868: Implementation of Recommendations of the Final Report on the Defense Science Board Task Force on the Design and Acquisition of Software for Defense Systems
FY19	Section 869: Implementation of Pilot Program to Use Agile or Iterative Development Methods Required Under Section 873 of the National Defense Authorization Act for Fiscal Year 2018
FY18	Section 872: Defense Innovation Board Analysis of Software Acquisition Regulations

Table 1.1—Continued

FY for NDAA	NDAA Provision
FY18	Section 873: Pilot Program to Use Agile or Iterative Development Methods to Tailor Major Software-Intensive Warfighting Systems and Defense Business Systems.
FY18	Section 874: Pilot Program to Use Agile or Iterative Development Methods to Tailor Major Software-Intensive Warfighting Systems and Defense Business Systems.
FY18	Section 891: Training on Agile or Iterative Development Methods.

SOURCE: Features information from DAU, "Software in NDAAs," undated-m.

- must demonstrate the viability and effectiveness of capabilities for operational use not later than one year after the date on which funds are first obligated
- must "use modern iterative software development methodologies (e.g., agile or lean), modern tools and techniques (e.g., development, security, and operations [DevSecOps]), and human-centered design processes to iteratively deliver software"[12]
- must employ active collaboration with end users
- must conduct value assessments at least annually[13]
- must leverage existing enterprise services
- must address cybersecurity, program protection, and intellectual property (IP) from program inception
- must integrate, streamline, and automate software development testing, government developmental testing, system safety assessment, security certification, and operational test and evaluation (T&E).[14]

---

[12] DoDI 5000.87, 2020, p. 4.

[13] According to DoDI 5000.87, a *value assessment* is "an outcome-based assessment of mission improvements and efficiencies realized from the delivered software capabilities, and a determination of whether the outcomes have been worth the investment. The sponsor and user community perform value assessments at least annually, to inform DA and [Program Manager] PM decisions" (DoDI 5000.87, 2020, p 23).

[14] DAU, undated-k; DoDI 5000.87, 2020, pp. 10–11.

The SWP is authorized pursuant to the FY20 NDAA, Section 800.[15] DoDI 5000.87 specifies that software acquired or developed using the authority under this section

> shall not be treated as a major defense acquisition program for purposes of section 2430 of title 10, U.S. Code, or Department of Defense Directive 5000.01 without the specific direction of the Under Secretary of Defense for Acquisition and Sustainment or a Senior Acquisition Executive.[16]

To assist with implementation, the DAU developed additional webpages on its AAF website, which is specifically devoted to the SWP.[17] The website provides helpful resources on SWP policies, statutory language, current SWP programs, basic information on the planning and execution phases, and such activities as

- creation of definitions of capability needs
- development of strategies
- cost estimation
- engagement with users and assessment of value
- MVP or MVCR and deployment
- architecture
- interoperability
- cybersecurity
- DevSecOps
- metrics and reporting.

The website includes continuous learning modules and resources that are relevant to the activity, templates for some of the artifacts and a Com-

---

[15] DAU commonly refers to the Software Acquisition Pathway with the abbreviation *SWP* in all of its AAF portal documentation.

[16] DAU, undated-f.

[17] DAU, undated-k.

munity of Interest,[18] and a vignette on experiences with SWP for an Army program.[19] In July 2020, DAU released an SWP quick-start guide that provides a high-level overview of what is needed to enter the planning phase and obtain subsequent entry into the execution phase.[20] As additional programs enter the pathway, they might benefit from a more comprehensive guidebook that is geared specifically toward the SWP.[21]

In April 2022, the Secretary of the Navy released Secretary of the Navy Instruction (SECNAVINST) 5000.2G regarding implementation of the AAF. It discusses the Navy's processes to integrate a program into the SWP.[22] The guidance provides PMs with the ability to tailor artifacts and choose their preferred management approaches once the minimum requirements set forth in DoDI 5000.87 are met. SECNAVINST 5000.2G also sets the minimum metrics that must be reported by the program.

Joint Cyber Weapons Acquisition Program

Marine Corps Systems Command's (MARCORSYSCOM's) Joint Cyber Weapons (JCW) acquisition program provides advanced cyberwarfare capabilities to support U.S. Marine Corps Forces Cyberspace Command, U.S. Cyber Command (USCYBERCOM), combatant commanders, and other federal government agencies' global operations. The capabilities delivered by the JCW program typically fall into three categories: exploits, implants, and payloads. All deliverables are common components of offensive cyber weapons that are developed to attack or exploit an adversary's systems vulnerabilities. According to MITRE's Common Attack Pattern

---

[18] The SWP Community of Interest is a forum in which different components collaborate to develop SWP policy.

[19] Sean Brady, "Adaptive Acquisition Framework (AAF) Vignette Middle Tier of Acquisition (MTA) and Software Acquisition Pathway (SWP) Hybrid," DAU, July 2022.

[20] DAU, *Software Acquisition Pathway Quick Start Primer*, undated-l.

[21] DAU, "Acquisition Guidebooks & References," webpage, undated-a.

[22] SECNAVINST 5000.2G, *Department of the Navy Implementation of the Defense Acquisition System and the Adaptive Acquisition Framework*, Office of the Secretary, Department of the Navy, April 8, 2022.

Enumeration and Classification (CAPEC) cyber terminology and taxonomy web portal, a *vulnerability* is

> a flaw in a software, firmware, hardware, or service component resulting from a weakness that can be exploited, causing a negative impact to the confidentiality, integrity, or availability of an impacted component or components.[23]

Exploits are software code that takes advantage of vulnerabilities to achieve a negative impact on the confidentiality, integrity, or availability of one or more system components.[24] *Implants* are software code that secures and maintains access to an adversary's system and is initially created by one or more exploits.[25] *Payloads* are software code that is capable of achieving the intended effect of a cyberattack.[26] The JCW program develops and delivers exploits, implants, and payloads in concert with other joint and uniformed services programs as part of the Joint Cyber Warfighting Architecture (JCWA), which is managed by USCYBERCOM.

The JCW program was created before the decision was made to induct it into the SWP. A September 2020 USCYBERCOM JCW Information System Initial Capabilities Document authorized the Marine Corps to develop requirements that the JCW program would implement. Following a merit-based assessment of the program for entry into the SWP in July 2021, the JCW program was designated for the planning phase of SWP in October 2021.[27] The first SWP-related acquisition artifact, the JCW Capability Needs Statement (CNS), was validated in July 2022.

---

[23] CAPEC, "CAPEC Glossary," webpage, MITRE Corporation, undated.

[24] CAPEC, undated.

[25] Lillian Ablon and Andy Bogart, *Zero Days, Thousands of Nights: The Life and Times of Zero-Day Vulnerabilities and Their Exploits*, RAND Corporation, RR-1751-RC, 2017.

[26] Steven M. Bellovin, Susan Landau, and Herbert S. Lin, "Limiting the Undesired Impact of Cyber Weapons: Technical Requirements and Policy Implications," *Journal of Cybersecurity*, Vol. 3, No. 1, March 2017.

[27] U.S. Marine Corps Systems Command, *Decision Memorandum for Joint Cyber Weapons: Payloads, Exploits, and Implants Program Use of the Software Acquisition Pathway and Entry into the Planning Phase*, October 22, 2021, Not available to the general public.

RAND was asked by MARCORSYSCOM to assist Marine Corps Cyberspace Operations with the following tasks:

- Develop the planning phase documentation for the JCW program.
- Conduct a Lifecycle Cost Estimate.
- Document user roles and responsibilities.
- Develop the Test Strategy, Information Support Plan (ISP), Product Support Strategy, and Cybersecurity Strategy.
- Tailor an Intellectual Property Strategy for the JCW program.

These acquisition artifacts are necessary to meet the requirements set forth for programs using the SWP within the AAF. DoD emphasized the necessity to implement the SWP in its February 2022 release of DoD's Software Modernization strategy.[28]

Approach

This report builds on prior RAND research from FY21 that brought together data on operational capability, scheduling, and risk to develop a life-cycle cost-estimating framework for the JCW program.[29] This framework helped JCW program leadership understand the potential costs and budgeting considerations of existing program lines of effort and alternative ways forward. The framework and its results were then applied during the planning phase of the SWP for the program. Also, in FY21, the JCW PM presented Commander, MARCORSYSCOM with the costs and benefits of using various pathways for the JCW program. Leadership ultimately agreed that the SWP would provide the best path for the JCW program as it progresses through its acquisition life cycle.

---

[28] U.S. Department of Defense, *Department of Defense Software Modernization Strategy*, version 1.0, November 2021b.

[29] Bradley Wilson, Thomas Goughnour, Megan McKernan, Andrew Karode, Devin Tierney, Mark V. Arena, Michael J. D. Vermeer, Hansell Perez, and Alexis Levedahl, *A Cost Estimating Framework for U.S. Marine Corps Joint Cyber Weapons*, RAND Corporation, RR-A1124-1, 2023.

Acquisition Program Artifacts

To enter the SWP execution phase, per DoD guidance, a program must have a Capability Need Statement, User Agreement, Acquisition Strategy, Test Strategy, and Cost Estimate.[30] These and other artifacts serve the following important functions:

- presenting the capabilities needed in the context of the threat environment (CNS)
- documenting the roles, responsibilities, needs, and commitment of various users of the capability (User Agreement)
- designing a road map to implement rapid fielding of user capabilities (Acquisition Strategy)
- estimating how much the program will cost (Cost Estimate)
- ensuring that the capabilities work in an operational environment (Test Strategy).[31]

Developing this documentation during the planning phase assists the program and various decisionmakers in several ways, including

- committing user involvement
- sharing information across the service and DoD
- providing the program with a plan to execute
- identifying ways to measure progress and documenting program changes.

We applied a multipronged methodology to completing these acquisition artifacts that consisted of a review of all relevant statutes, regulations, and policy, along with other program documentation prepared for such purposes as market research or budget justifications; discussions with key stakeholders in the requirements, acquisition, and user communities; and the development of a detailed schedule to track important deadlines and coordination points.

---

[30] DoDI 5000.87, 2020.

[31] In the case of JCW, the program is tested in an isolated environment that mirrors an operational environment.

Limitations

The issues identified in this report are based on our experience during development of SWP acquisition artifacts for the JCW program. Lessons cannot necessarily be extrapolated to other programs. However, we attempt to identify lessons that might be of interest to other programs that adhere to the SWP.

The JCW program was initiated prior to the SWP. Following an assessment, the Marine Corps determined that the SWP was the most appropriate for JCW. The program had to pivot to different acquisition artifact requirements as a result. Some of the issues that we identify might be byproducts of the pivot, and might not apply to programs intending to start on SWP from inception.

Structure of this Report

In Chapter Two, we discuss what we consider to be the major lessons that we learned while producing acquisition artifacts for the JCW acquisition program during the planning phase. In the appendix, we provide a description and lessons learned on the specific artifacts developed to assist the JCW program office as it navigated the planning phase and prepared for the execution phase of the SWP.

CHAPTER 2

Insights

From our experiences assisting with the SWP artifacts for the JCW program, we were able to glean some insights that might be beneficial for other programs. In this chapter, we discuss the overall lessons that we learned and recommendations that emerged from our experiences.

Prioritizing the Acquisition Artifact Development Schedule Is Necessary to Meet Planning Phase Timelines

The JCW Product Manager devised an acquisition artifact schedule for the software pathway planning phase that coincided with source selection and subsequent contract award. In this case, one year was the stated goal of the schedule. In a July 2022 briefing, the Office of the Secretary of Defense (OSD) noted that about 50 percent of SWP programs spent no more than six months in the planning phase, which reflects an aggressive artifact schedule for the SWP.[1] A detailed schedule of all artifacts, milestones, and coordination and review periods were added to the schedule. Every two weeks, there was a review that included discussions of any challenges in drafting the planning artifacts. The program office, requirements community, and the user community prioritized the schedule. Data needs were addressed as much as was feasible, and adjustments were made to the schedule so that progress could be made on one artifact if another was stalled for any reason.

---

[1] Sean Brady, "DoD's Software Acquisition Pathway, Digital Delivery at the Speed of Relevance," DAU—Let's Talk Agile briefing, July 27, 2022.

Because of this attention to the schedule, the JCW program was on schedule for its artifacts for the planning phase.

Recommendations for Artifact Schedule Prioritization

When prioritizing an artifact development schedule, proactive trades will need to be made between documentation completeness, content depth, and getting "good enough" documentation in the hands of decisionmakers. For example, the artifacts were not perfect, but they did contain adequate information to move to the execution phase with the understanding that they were "living" documents that would need to be revised during execution. Similarly, a decision was made to draft the artifacts concurrently. By doing so, the schedule was prioritized over producing the artifacts sequentially, which likely would have been an easier but longer process. In addition, the program office worked with a federally funded research and development center that was tasked with pulling together the planning documentation in close collaboration with the program office staff. Having dedicated staff with subject-matter expertise also helped keep the planning phase on schedule. Future efforts will need to ensure that adequate staff are available to pull together the planning artifacts. It was clear that the program office did not have sufficient staff for all the required planning period tasks. Because the SWP was new, it was also not easy to judge how much staff time would be required to perform every task concurrently. Assuming that the study team's experience on this project is representative of future programs and because of how quickly the artifacts need to be produced, any documentation that requires discussion on dependencies between programs (e.g., ISP) is likely to be challenging to produce on time. It is also important for stakeholders to understand that the artifacts will need to be updated over the course of the program life cycle.

An additional challenge that slowed down some of the effort included the sequential signing off on documents, which is the norm in DoD's structure. The sign-off was a significant portion of the overall time needed to develop the acquisition artifacts. Sign-off took one to three months, roughly 20 to 60 percent of the total artifact time, while authoring took three to five months.[2] Although this is a significant percentage, it is a short amount of time relative to sign-off in the more traditional acquisition path. Discussions of content and issues while documents were being drafted helped prepare stakeholders for sign-off with minimal delays.

Finally, a classification guide is essential in the preplanning stage to make sure that content is accurately labeled during the writing phase and to minimize the need to rework later. This is particularly true for both offensive and defensive cyber capabilities because of both the high classifications of some of the details and the evolving levels of classification. We found numerous instances of content in program documentation from several years earlier that was later reclassified at lower levels in more recent program documentation. The lack of authoritative guidance was a key factor in drafting and submitting the ISP for classification review on the Joint Worldwide Intelligence Communication System (JWICS), for example, even though the main document was intended to be CUI.

Early and Ongoing Coordination Between Stakeholders Is Beneficial for the Program

Stakeholder coordination is a key factor in maintaining the schedule priority for the SWP.[3] In March 2022, the U.S. Government Accountability Office (GAO) reported that leading companies "solicit early feedback from customers for both hardware and software development" to develop a sound business case.[4] In March 2019, GAO also stated that "previous GAO reports as well as other DoD and industry studies have also found that user involve-

---

[2] It is unlikely these durations can be used for or extrapolated to other programs due to the unknown and often unique factors that drive programs.

[3] It is also worth noting here that the frequency of stakeholder coordination in agile development methodologies is a cost consideration during earlier phases of the program (such as in development of the User Agreement) and recurs as user requirements evolve. The nature of both the operational environment and the capabilities demanded by users makes this particularly applicable to offensive cyber capabilities.

[4] GAO, *Leading Practices: Agency Acquisition Policies Could Better Implement Key Product Development Principles*, March 10, 2022, p. 21.

ment is critical to the success of any software development effort."[5] According to GAO, early and continual engagement is a key characteristic of effective user engagement.[6]

The requirements, user, and acquisition communities need to be in agreement on key issues and share an understanding of timelines, roles, and responsibilities. The User Agreement is an important input to the software pathway because "active user engagement" is a key tenet of the pathway.[7] The roles of Product Manager and Lead User Representative were very important roles for the JCW program because close communication between these officials provided the DAs with adequate and timely information to approve the artifacts.

Recommendations for Coordination

Establishing coordination mechanisms early in the planning phase is important for work to be seamless between stakeholders. This coordination will help mitigate any risks to the planning phase schedule. User representatives with significant experience in the subject matter should be appointed to work as key stakeholders with the acquisition staff.

Tailoring Is a Key Tool for Drafting Useful Software Acquisition Pathway Artifacts

Tailoring of acquisition artifacts to fit the uniqueness of the program should also be a top planning consideration. This could be challenging because authors might not have the experience to know which elements of an artifact template are relevant.[8] There were many discussions within the pro-

---

[5] GAO, *DoD Space Acquisitions: Including Users Early and Often in Software Development Could Benefit Programs*, March 18, 2019, p. 11. Note also that this should not be considered a new insight.

[6] GAO, 2019, p. 23.

[7] DAU, "Active User Engagement," webpage, undated-c; DAU, undated-k.

[8] Appendix J of DoD Standard Practice MIL-STD-881F could be useful for providing a framework for tailoring acquisition documentation using the work breakdown

gram office about how tailoring should be done to produce not only what the program needed for successful execution but also the minimum content needed to provide the DA and other stakeholders with adequate oversight over the program. DoD's guidance for operation of the SWP calls for tailoring the Acquisition Strategy and related program documentation "to what is needed to effectively manage the program."[9] DoD and Navy guidance make the program's DA responsible for approving document tailoring approaches.[10] The ISP that the study team developed is an example of program documentation being specifically tailored to the characteristics of the JCW program, its relationships to other programs and architectures, and where the JCW program was in its life cycle.

Recommendations for Tailoring Acquisition Artifacts

In a 2015 RAND report, McKernan, Drezner, and Sollinger stated that "tailoring is part of careful and effective program planning."[11] According to this research, urgent requirements provided "a strong incentive for tailoring" but demanded an acquisition workforce and leadership that could implement such an approach.[12] In a 2022 RAND report, Wong et al. found that

> to achieve desirable acquisition outcomes, acquisition strategies . . . must be tailorable to the unique characteristics of each program. There is no one-size-fits-all approach that works with every program, and attempts to force programs into a single paradigm lead to problems and inefficiencies.[13]

---

structure of their programs (DoD Standard Practice MIL-STD-881F, Work Breakdown Structures for Defense Material Items, U.S. Department of Defense, May 13, 2022).

[9] DoDI 5000.87, 2020, p. 11.

[10] See DoDI 5000.87, 2020, and SECNAVINST 5000.2G, 2022.

[11] Megan McKernan, Jeffrey A. Drezner, and Jerry M. Sollinger, *Tailoring the Acquisition Process in the U.S. Department of Defense*, RAND Corporation, RR-966-OSD, 2015, p. 34.

[12] McKernan Drezner, and Sollinger, 2015, p. 46.

[13] Jonathan P. Wong, Obaid Younossi, Christine Kistler LaCoste, Philip S. Anton, Alan J. Vick, Guy Weichenberg, and Thomas C. Whitmore , *Improving Defense Acquisi-*

Effective tailoring requires leadership support and critical thinking on what is applicable to the program. These discussions should happen up front and often as the artifacts are being drafted. Tailoring should also be explicitly called out in acquisition artifacts so that the DA can understand the risks involved in failing to address certain parts of the artifacts. Maintaining a log of artifact sections and topic areas and which were removed or altered is a good practice. Finally, good examples of signed documentation from other programs would be helpful as DoD's workforce tackles this new acquisition pathway.[14]

Leverage the User Agreement to Define Stakeholder Roles and Relationships in the Software Process

We found the User Agreement to be the most appropriate SWP artifact to define stakeholder roles and relationships in the software process with respect to agility in managing requirements changes. Users are key stakeholders in defining high-level needs, and those needs drive the requirements that the software is developed to meet. The agreement defined the relationships in the process between users, the sponsor, the PM, the product manager, development teams, and development and operational testers.

We also found that segmenting high-level needs into needs statements, to be approved by high-level stakeholders, would seek to keep the requirements definition at a reasonable scope (i.e., not too detailed). The needs statements could then be further defined into more-detailed functional level declarations at the working level, so that they could be given to software developers to implement. The functional-level declarations are more easily changeable at the working level.[15]

---

tion: *Insights from Three Decades of RAND Research*, RAND Corporation, RR-A1670-1, 2022, p. vi.

[14] The desire for access to approved artifact examples from other programs has also emerged during other (ongoing) RAND research.

[15] This is supported by other (ongoing and previous) RAND research efforts.

The capabilities delivered by the JCW program are less likely to be typical of the software applications that the authors of DoDI 5000.87 had in mind because the capabilities usually do not start small and continuously deliver capability into the hands of users. However, every other service's cyber component program office has incorporated agile methods and Development and Operations (DevOps) or DevSecOps into their offensive cyber capability development process.[16] Offensive cyber capability development might become an important demonstration case for SWP because of the potential variety of urgency,[17] size,[18] duration,[19] and complexity of the capabilities involved.[20]

Recommendations for User Agreements

Establish an adaptive and continuous requirements management process in the User Agreement for the management and translation of high-level capability needs into functional requirements, software development, and testing.

---

[16] Agile Alliance, homepage, undated; Gartner, "Information Technology Gartner Glossary," webpage, undated; Manifesto for Agile Software Development, homepage, undated; U.S. Department of Defense, *DoD Enterprise DevSecOps Reference Design*, version 1.0, August 12, 2019. It is worth noting that agile development methods and DevOps and DevSecOps are complementary but not identical. DevOps and DevSecOps are approaches to aligning the work of software development, operations, and (for DevSecOps in particular) security teams that can be applied to any software development process, not just agile ones.

[17] Urgency can vary from immediate to deliberate.

[18] In terms of source lines of code, size can vary from relatively modest exploits, implants, and payloads to substantial toolkits and effects chains.

[19] Duration can vary from short-lifespan one-off capabilities to more-enduring capabilities with a sustainment life cycle.

[20] Complexity can vary from software-only to complex multisystem or multicomponent mixed hardware-software effects chains.

Current Software Acquisition Pathway Templates Do Not Consider Offensive Cyber Software

This insight is logical because offensive cyber capabilities are a niche type of software relative to the vast quantities of code written to provide other services in DoD and considering the newness of the SWP. However, it is worthwhile for policymakers to think about how offensive cyber software differs from the types of software that the authors of SWP policy envisioned and to leave flexibility in the pathway for alternate, shorter-lifespan or variable-lifespan software.

Recommendations for Offensive Cyber Artifact Templates

OSD should consider developing modified guidance and reporting metrics for cyber weapon SWP programs because they are significantly different forms of software from typical continuously operated systems.

Stakeholder Artifact Approvals Were Expeditious

One area that often burdens traditional acquisition programs is getting approval on acquisition artifacts, such as requirements from myriad stakeholders. The JCW's artifact sign-off approach was expeditious; typically stakeholders approved in a few months. This was partly because SWP provides useful flexibility to programs in pushing approvals down to the most-appropriate echelons and because the JCW program was not seeking broad consensus approval. Because of this flexibility, the program was willing to be more risk tolerant knowing that the SWP artifacts are living documents and can be changed as needed in the future. Successful testing and approvals are still warranted however, to ensure buy-in from appropriate stakeholders.

Preplanning Can Lack Information to Inform a Reasonable Scope of Software Acquisition Pathway Artifacts

The SWP guidance permits programs to create stand-alone artifacts for the various information requirements for the programs (e.g., contracting, testing, IP, product support) or to cover these topics in the Acquisition Strategy. What would be acceptable for the DA is determined prior to the start of the planning phase. At that point, there is a general understanding of various parts of the Acquisition Strategy, but there is not always sufficient knowledge to fully understand whether it makes sense to develop a more detailed stand-alone artifact for the core parts of the Acquisition Strategy.

In the case of the JCW program, in consultation with the program office, the DA set the program on a path for developing documentation for nine artifacts (not including the Acquisition Strategy) during the planning phase. In hindsight, only two of those nine artifacts (the cost estimate and the CNS) had enough information available in preplanning to warrant a stand-alone artifact.

Recommendations for Preplanning

Focus solely on the Acquisition Strategy as the first acquisition artifact, and only create separate artifacts when sufficient information or circumstances warrant doing so. If a program is trying to move fast in the SWP, trying to generate numerous stand-alone artifacts in planning will be challenging. Some artifacts refer to or depend on content from others, but the research involved in collecting content for the Acquisition Strategy should help inform the scope and depth of additional artifacts that might be required and the phasing of their development.

Conclusions and Discussion

Because of the relatively recent availability of training through the DAU and service-level guidance in SECNAVINST 5000.2G, which was issued in

April 2022 and includes the SWP, programs still have a considerable learning curve to implement SWP guidance. DoD established SWP because prior processes did not explicitly incorporate modern approaches to software development, were planning intensive, and were not focused on incrementally delivering software. These findings were illustrated in a May 2019 DIB report and February 2018 DSB report.[21] Congress then included requirements in NDAAs for FY18 through FY20 for DoD to change its approach to software development.[22]

Additional direction to PMs could assist with implementing the SWP. For example, for the User Agreement, the guidance available on DAU's AAF site, in DODI 5000.87, or in SECNAVINST 5000.2G does not specify the authorities of a lead user representative, how that individual is to be chosen, and whether the lead user representative is also a user. The team found it difficult to define the lead user representative role without such guidance.

Policy guidance and training alone cannot change culture within the acquisition community, which has been accustomed to a process that was not tailored specifically to modern software practices. The pressure on programs to quickly turn around acquisition artifacts is high because of the importance placed on delivering software to the warfighter and transitioning to the execution phase. As a result of this pressure, programs risk producing artifacts that are not fully understood or leveraged by program officials. Programs can help mitigate these risks by

- prioritizing the acquisition artifact schedule
- ensuring early and ongoing stakeholder communication
- tailoring artifacts to meet program needs
- resourcing the program effectively to accomplish these tasks.

Despite the challenges faced by the JCW program office in preparing for the execution phase, the program office successfully pulled together the appropriate SWP artifacts—within the goal of one year—to align with

---

[21] DIB, "Who Cares: Why Does Software Matter for DoD?," in *Software Acquisition and Practices (SWAP) Study Main Report*, U.S. Department of Defense, May 2019a; DSB, 2018.

[22] See Table 1.1 for more information.

source selection using the key insights outlined previously. It would be beneficial to do a retrospective assessment after the JCW program has been in the execution phase for a period of time to capture additional lessons learned related to

- the usefulness of the artifacts in educating stakeholders and informing program decisions
- the utility of the metrics laid out in the Acquisition Strategy
- how and to what extent SWP policy guidance and management processes might have evolved and the effect of any changes on the artifacts
- the extent to which the artifacts continue to be maintained, useful management tools.

In this report, we have documented eight insights from our multiyear effort supporting the Marine Corps Cyberspace Operations program office that we hope will inform this and other programs as they embark on the journey down the SWP. Of course, the portion of the above recommendations that would be feasible to implement, in terms of scope and pace, is also a function of how a Program Management Office (PMO) is organized and resourced, to what degree the program can be or has been tailored in its work breakdown structure and documentation requirements, and with which other programs it might be expected to coordinate or synchronize. For example, at the time of this writing, there were ongoing efforts to better align Service Cyber Component program execution under the JCWA led by a program executive office within USCYBERCOM. How these efforts evolve, where they end up, and what resources are committed to each PMO will likely shape which of the insights and recommendations described in this report can be realistically implemented by a PMO.

Specific Joint Cyber Weapon Program Artifacts Lessons Learned

In this appendix, we provide descriptions of and additional lessons learned about the specific artifacts that were developed to assist the JCW program office as it navigates the planning phase and prepares for the execution phase of the SWP. Steps involved in the planning and execution phases for programs in the SWP are detailed in DoDI 5000.87, sections 3.2 and 3.3, respectively. Additional guidance is provided on DAU's AAF internet portal.[1] The two documents required for entry to the SWP planning phase (per DoDI 5000.87) are an Acquisition Decision Memorandum (ADM) signed by the DA authorizing use of SWP and a draft CNS. The draft CNS informs the planning phase and outlines key decisions, including program sponsorship, structure of the program (new PMO versus existing PMO or program alignment), and the Acquisition Strategy. Whether other artifacts beyond the Acquisition Strategy are needed (or advisable) are determined by the PM in coordination with applicable DAs. All these artifacts may also be tailored to suit the circumstances of the program.

Acquisition Strategy

Major acquisition programs are statutorily required to develop an Acquisition Strategy,[2] but this strategy development is also required by DoD policy

---

[1] DAU, undated-l.

[2] "(a) Acquisition Strategy Required. There shall be an acquisition strategy for each major defense acquisition program, each major automated information system, and

for SWP programs.[3] A program's Acquisition Strategy is the central location of key summary program information for decisionmakers, including the following:

- the proposed top-level business and technical management approach for the program or system
- an explanation of how the strategy is designed to be implemented with available resources
- how the strategy is tailored to address program requirements and constraints
- incremental delivery of capability
- use of mature technology
- future capability improvements
- industrial base considerations
- risk management
- business strategy
- contracting strategy
- Intellectual Property Strategy
- international involvement
- multiyear procurement
- integration of current intelligence assessments into the acquisition process
- requirements related to logistics, maintenance, and sustainment.[4]

The AAF tailors this information requirement to what DoD is acquiring through each acquisition pathway. In the past, DoD's acquisition policy sought to obtain knowledge on technologies, product design, and manufacturing processes using an evolutionary system development that separated

---

each major system approved by a milestone decision authority" (U.S. Code, Title 10, Subtitle A, Part V, Subpart F, Chapter 322, Subchapter 1, Section 4211, Acquisition Strategy). The Acquisition Strategy is a regulatory requirement for other programs and includes statutory and regulatory information on the acquisition program.

[3] "PMs will develop and execute an approved acquisition strategy." (DoDI 5000.87, 2020, Section 3.2.d[1]).

[4] U.S. Code, Title 10, Section 4211.

technology from system development.[5] However, there needed to be more flexibility to allow programs to operate agilely and encourage iteration to be built into requirements development, acquisition, and fielding of software. As a result, the AAF was designed to "empower PMs; delegate decisions; tailor in processes; and focus on data driven decisions" for the multitude of capabilities that DoD acquires (including the intricacies of software acquisition).[6]

Within the AAF, the SWP "values working software over comprehensive documentation."[7] DoD guidance for operation of the SWP defines the Acquisition Strategy as "an integrated plan that identifies the overall approach to rapidly and iteratively acquire, develop, deliver, and sustain software capabilities to meet the users' needs."[8] The Acquisition Strategy is required for a program to enter the SWP execution phase, but the Acquisition Strategy is updated throughout the program's life cycle. The Acquisition Strategy is intended to be tailorable to "what is needed to effectively manage the program."[9] However, DoD guidance provides "key elements of the [software] Acquisition Strategy":

    a. Risk-based business and technical management approach to rapidly and iteratively deliver software capabilities balanced against quality, security, intelligence threats, system safety, performance, and other factors.

    b. Roadmap and cadence for software deliveries to operations including:

        1. Demonstrating the viability and effectiveness of capabilities for operational use not later than 1 year after the date on which funds are first obligated.

        2. Continuously delivering capabilities to operations at least annually thereafter.

---

[5] GAO, *Defense Acquisitions: Major Weapon Systems Continue to Experience Cost and Schedule Problems under DOD's Revised Policy*, April 13, 2006.

[6] DAU, undated-f.

[7] DAU, undated-f.

[8] DoDI 5000.87, 2020, p. 11.

[9] DoDI 5000.87, 2020, p. 11.

   3. If using the embedded software path, aligning and integrating with the development and fielding for the systems in which the software is embedded.

   c. Flexible and modular contract strategy that enables software development teams to rapidly design, develop, test, integrate, deploy, and support software capabilities.

   d. Planned use of government personnel and resources for software activities.

   e. Tailoring of acquisition processes to adopt modern software development practices (e.g., lean, agile, DevSecOps).

   f. Planned use of existing enterprise services, infrastructure, and resources.

   g. High level test strategies, coordinated with the T&E community, to validate software quality, integration and automation of testing, along with planned test platforms, resources, and infrastructure.

   h. Architecture strategies to enable a modular open systems approach that is interoperable with required systems.

   i. Cybersecurity strategies in accordance with the applicable cybersecurity policies and issuances which include recurring assessment of the supply chain, development environment, processes and tools, continuous automated cybersecurity test and operational evaluation to provide a system resilient to offensive cyber operations.

   j. IP, training, and product support strategies; and records management requirements in accordance with the appropriate DoDIs to ensure lifecycle supportability.

   k. The PM's strategy to ensure that the program is conducted in accordance with all applicable laws and regulations (e.g., Division E of Public Law 104-106, safety, sustainment, communication waveform management and standardization, and airworthiness) throughout the lifecycle.[10]

DoDI 5000.87 permits program offices to address certain statutory and regulatory requirements for the SWP in the Acquisition Strategy as opposed

---

[10] DoDI 5000.87, 2020, pp. 11–12.

to creating stand-alone artifacts for each core area of focus (e.g., cost estimate, IP, product support).

The JCW acquisition program office sought to develop an Acquisition Strategy to acquire needed cyberspace capabilities while taking into account resources and risks. The Acquisition Strategy creates the most comprehensive artifact to guide the program to the execution phase. The following aspects were identified as challenging during the planning and drafting of the JCW Acquisition Strategy:

1. planning for stand-alone JCW artifacts versus planning for a summary within the Acquisition Strategy
2. having sufficient information up front to address the respective parts of the Acquisition Strategy
3. applying certain parts of the Acquisition Strategy guidance to the JCW program, along with acceptable tailoring
4. concurrently writing the individual parts of the Acquisition Strategy.

Planning for Standalone versus Summary Documentation

SWP guidance permits programs to create stand-alone artifacts for the various information requirements for the programs (e.g., contracting, testing, IP, product support) or these topics can be covered in the Acquisition Strategy.[11] The decision for what would be acceptable for the DA is made prior to the start of the planning phase. At that point, there is a general understanding of various parts of the Acquisition Strategy, but there is not sufficient knowledge to fully understand whether it makes sense to develop a more detailed stand-alone artifact for the core parts of the Acquisition Strategy. In the case of the JCW program, in consultation with the program office,

---

[11] In this context, *stand-alone* refers to a document with content that has sufficient scope, level of detail, and context such that it can stand on its own as a reference without the need for the reader to turn to other documents for additional but necessary details. This objective means that stand-alone reference documentation tends to lead to some duplication of content between documents.

the DA sets the program on a path for developing documentation for the following stand-alone artifacts during the planning phase:[12]

- CNS[13]
- User Agreement[14]
- Acquisition Strategy
- Cybersecurity Strategy
- Test Strategy
- Intellectual Property Strategy
- Product Support Strategy
- ISP
- Program Cost Estimate
- Clinger Cohen Act (CCA) Compliance.

The JCW program office prepared the documentation as requested but found that, because of the uniqueness of the JCW program and software generally, the program office struggled with creating a stand-alone document for the Cybersecurity Strategy and an ISP; the other documents struggled to sufficiently define the scope in enough detail to warrant a stand-alone document.

The Acquisition Strategy template must include information from the User Agreement, Test Strategy, Cybersecurity Strategy, Capability Need Statement, Intellectual Property Strategy, and ISP. A DAU training session noted that "some of these sections may be stand-alone documents and simply summarized in the Acquisition Strategy."[15] Additional guidance and examples could help programs navigate how much information should be included from these stand-alone documents into the Acquisition Strategy or even whether a stand-alone document is required at all. This might help avoid unnecessary duplication across documents. Better understanding

---

[12] U.S. Marine Corps Systems Command, 2021.

[13] The CNS was developed by the requirements community, but the JCW program office coordinated.

[14] The JCW program office partnered with the user community to develop the User Agreement.

[15] Brady, 2021, p. 63.

this approach could also help programs plan for the extent to which they will need to synchronize changes across documents that are being developed simultaneously. Doing so would ensure that the Acquisition Strategy reflects other stand-alone documents when those documents move through approval processes at differing speeds.

Having Sufficient Information Up Front to Address the Respective Parts of the Acquisition Strategy

For the JCW program, the amount of information available during the software planning phase led to areas in which there was less depth of knowledge to address all parts of the Acquisition Strategy. For example, the section on metrics included the full set of metrics that OSD requests semiannually, but the program office was not able to do a full assessment during the planning phase to understand what metrics could or could not be pulled together using existing program staff and resources.[16] A baseline for the risks that the program might face was established but will likely need an update. Similarly, the program's assessment of value was also a starting point; this assessment might change depending on user feedback. These examples point to the importance of treating these documents as living documents that should be updated when new information is available rather than at milestones like in traditional acquisition programs.

Applying Certain Parts of the Acquisition Strategy Guidance to the Program, Along with Acceptable Tailoring

The Acquisition Strategy contains a wide variety of information. Given the uniqueness of the JCW program, it was difficult to discern what content to keep in the Acquisition Strategy and what to tailor out. Without additional guidance on tailoring and examples of adequate program documentation, the program office erred on the side of retaining content when unsure of its value to the program.

---

[16] DAU, "Program Management Metrics and Reporting," webpage, undated-j.

Some sections of the Acquisition Strategy do not clearly link to articulating a plan "to rapidly and iteratively acquire, develop, deliver, and sustain software capabilities to meet the users' needs."[17] The Acquisition Strategy template requires information on software development approaches. New programs could find some utility in describing how their current or planned process compares with stated software acquisition methodologies. However, existing programs, when describing processes that are already in place, should consider both the reference and education value for current and future staff as an argument for including such content. That said, senior decisionmakers who are unfamiliar with these software development approach descriptions might not find them helpful to understanding a plan to achieve the intended outcomes of the software acquisition. Because of these issues, additional guidance regarding tailoring is needed so that programs can address these issues according to their needs.

Concurrently Writing Individual Parts of the Acquisition Strategy

One of the main goals of the SWP is to reduce the time to fielding of the capability releases, so the user receives capability and can therefore provide valuable feedback for improvement in cycles of less than one year. The JCW program office created a goal of the planning phase for approximately one year to synchronize with source selection and also to ensure that the capability is delivered as quickly as possible. This schedule necessitated that all the requirements and acquisition documentation be drafted concurrently with a final goal of summarizing the pieces in the Acquisition Strategy. The simultaneous drafting of all this documentation required much effort to standardize messaging and reduce potential errors during review, coordination, and approval. The end result was a sufficient plan to move forward to the execution phase with the assumption that pieces of the artifacts would need to be updated during the execution phase. The effort required in the drafting of the documentation is partly why we recommend developing only the Acquisition Strategy when there is minimal information at the start of the SWP planning phase.

---

[17] DAU, "Acquisition Strategy," webpage, undated-b.

Cybersecurity Strategy

With the implementation of the AAF, DoD revised its cybersecurity guidance for acquisition programs to account for DoD's new approach to managing acquisitions. DoD emphasized the importance of cybersecurity in its policy guidance for the SWP and across all pathways in the AAF. DoDI 5000.87 states that

> software assurance, cyber security, test and evaluation are integral parts of this [risk-based management] approach to continually assess and measure cyber security preparedness and responsiveness, identify and address risks and execute mitigation actions.[18]

According to guidance from the DoD Chief Information Officer, the Cybersecurity Strategy "outlines plans for, and implementation status of, projected cybersecurity activities across all phases of a system's lifecycle."[19] DoD guidance notes that the Cybersecurity Strategy is a living document that will be updated throughout the life cycle of a program.

To address requirements for its Cybersecurity Strategy, the JCW program sought to characterize the threat and describe the program's approach to stakeholder communication, system engineering management, operations management, system design and architecture, requirements traceability, risk assessments, implementation, operations and sustainment, etc. Because of the uniqueness of the cybertools developed by the JCW program, the Cybersecurity Strategy needed to be tailorable and flexible.

Despite existing guidance, the following were challenges developing JCW's Cybersecurity Strategy:

- There was insufficient clarity around what specific information would be needed in a Cybersecurity Strategy artifact to support decisionmaking for the SWP.
- The directed document template was not intended for SWP programs.

---

[18] DoDI 5000.87, 2020, p. 4.

[19] U.S. Department of Defense, *Cybersecurity Strategy Outline and Guidance*, June 24, 2021a, p. 2.

- There was uncertainty around the level of detail required for a program prior to the execution phase.
- The threat baseline used was not specific to the types of threats JCW was likely to face.

These challenges are discussed in more detail in the sections that follow.

Insufficient Clarity Around What Information Was Needed to Support Decisionmaking for the Software Acquisition Pathway

It was unclear what specific information would be needed in a Cybersecurity Strategy artifact for decisionmakers in the SWP. Other artifacts were better supported by clearer guidance from OSD (e.g., Acquisition Strategy). Without clearer guidance at the OSD level, the JCW program office used guidance from SECNAVINST 5000.2G and DAU's AAF SWP internet portal for programs using the AAF, which included a template of the artifact.[20]

Using Templates That Are Not Designed for Software Acquisition Pathway Artifacts

As the review process started for the Cybersecurity Strategy, the JCW program office was initially directed to use a template that was not designed for SWP programs. Although the template used might have been more familiar to the reviewers, several sections did not appear to be applicable to the SWP. Even when using the template designed for SWP programs, a level of tailoring was necessary. For example, information was required on JCIDS-related documentation despite the program following the Cyber Capabilities Integration and Development System. However, it was unclear to what extent tailoring was encouraged in the Cybersecurity Strategy. As a result,

---

[20] "[Cybersecurity Strategies] CSSs sent to [Department of the Navy] DON [Chief Information Officer] CIO for review shall conform with the DoD Cybersecurity Strategy Outline and Guidance published on the DAU website . . . . The DoD CSS. Outline and Guidance is applicable to all AAF pathways, and retains operational relevance beyond milestone decisions into system sustainment" (SECNAVINST 5000.2G, p. 2).

the JCW program office attempted to adhere as closely to the DAU guidance as possible.

Uncertainty in the Level of Detail Needed Prior to Execution Phase

The JCW program office was unsure of what level of detail was required for a program prior to its execution phase. Because of the detail asked for by the instructions, the strategy seemed more appropriate for a program that was further along in operational status than the JCW program was or most SWP programs would be. Subsequently, the intent of the cyber strategy was kept broad and focused on best practices in general rather than the specific boundaries of the JCW program. The JCW acquisition program contracts were some of the foundational references that were used to glean which requirements were put in place regarding cybersecurity as it pertained to the contractors performing the work on the JCW program. The contracts mainly focused on facilities and clearances (i.e., aspects of security) rather than information security requirements of technical infrastructure. According to the GAO, a Cybersecurity Strategy is "intended to help ensure that program staff are planning for and documenting cybersecurity risk management efforts, which begin early in the programs' life cycle."[21] This is another reason why we recommend focusing only on the Acquisition Strategy in these instances in which there is limited information to support a stand-alone artifact.

Use of a Generic Threat Baseline Not Tailored to the Program's Operating Environment

The Cybersecurity Strategy included a characterization of the threat that was not based on a comprehensive stand-alone threat assessment conducted by the program. The threat characterization section was based on open-source research and informed by known general threats. Using a specific threat assessment as the foundation for the section might have yielded more

---

[21] GAO, *Software Development: DoD Faces Risks and Challenges in Implementing Modern Approaches and Addressing Cybersecurity Practices*, June 23, 2021a, p. 36.

relevant and current information. Such an assessment is not required as part of the SWP. Therefore, it is unlikely that programs would devote resources to conducting such assessments, considering the numerous artifacts that require their attention and resources.

Programs should be prepared to update their Cybersecurity Strategy later in the program life cycle. Direct discussions with developers in the subsequent steps of the program might help fill in the gaps. Additional guidance from cybersecurity experts and access to a tailored artifact or guidance that is better aligned with the SWP might also yield more appropriately tailored cybersecurity for the JCW program.

Intellectual Property Strategy

DoD has known that IP is inseparable from the Acquisition Strategy for defense programs.[22] However, sophisticated management and oversight of IP has been lacking because of the technical nature of IP practice, the variation in the types of acquisition programs across DoD, and several complicated implications for IP across the acquisition life cycle. Congress began to address this need in the 2018 NDAA by instructing DoD to create an IP Cadre—a team of experts in IP acquisition, policy, and strategy—that would serve as a departmentwide resource to help acquisition managers understand and plan for their IP needs.[23] DoD responded with DoDI 5010.44, which not only established DoD's policy that "[a]cquiring and licensing the appropriate IP is vital for ensuring the systems will remain functional, sustainable, upgradable and affordable" but also stated that each component was to appoint one or more offices with the responsibility for working closely with the new DoD IP Cadre to ensure that Component IP acquisition needs were consistent with DoD policy.[24] Since the passage of the 2018 NDAA and the issuance of DoDI 5101.44, DoD created the new IP Cadre and began reviewing IP needs across the Components. According to a 2021

---

[22] Pub. L. 115–91, 2017.

[23] Pub. L 115–91, 2017, Section 802.

[24] DoDI 5010.44, *Intellectual Property (IP) Acquisition and Licensing*, October 16, 2019.

GAO report, "[i]n an April 2020 report to Congress, DOD identified that it plans to publish a new department-wide IP guidebook intended to explain IP-related regulations and policies."[25]

Despite these initial actions to institutionalize the IP needs of the Departments and Components, concrete guidance and an overarching IP strategy have not yet emerged from the IP Cadre's activities. The aforementioned GAO report found that "DoD has not yet detailed how the IP Cadre will provide program support, [or] how the IP Cadre will provide two key areas of expertise, and future funding and staffing needs for the IP Cadre."[26] As of August 2022, the IP Cadre had not released guidance on creating IP strategies that would assist PMs in identifying IP needs, crafting approaches for IP licensing and other acquisitions, or incorporating flexible contracting strategies that would meet the DoD policy goals of a "functional, sustainable, upgradable, and affordable" IP acquisition approach.

As we developed the JCW Intellectual Property Strategy, the following observations emerged from the lacunae in DoD guidance:

- Marine Corps acquisition managers and contracting support have little direction on how to strategically manage the IP dimensions of their programs
- JCW's default licensing terms helped mitigate the lack of clear IP guidance from DoD
- A lack of practical IP guidance put JCW at a contracting disadvantage early in its life cycle.

The Need for Practical IP Guidance for Acquisition Managers and Contracting

Broad policy pronouncements, such as those contained in DoDI 5101.44 and the software-acquisition-specific DoDI 5000.87, set lofty but technically unmoored aspirations for IP licensing and purchases. For example, DoDI 5000.87 states that for the acquisition of software-based programs

---

[25] GAO, *Defense Acquisitions: DoD Should Take Additional Actions to Improve How it Approaches Intellectual Property*, November 30, 2021b, p. 17.

[26] GAO, 2021b, p. 21.

[t]he IP strategy will include, to the maximum extent practicable, negotiation for and periodic delivery of: all executables, source code, associated scripts, build procedures, automation scripts, tools, databases, libraries, test results, data sets, firmware, training materials, and any other elements necessary to integrate, test and evaluate, debug, deploy, and operate the software application in all relevant environments (e.g., development, staging, and production). Data sets and records should include those that support operations and mission-related decisions. Furthermore, it should address delivery of all software components where the government will have rights to the source code, such as open-source software and software developed at government expense; and a list of all third-party software components included in the software. The delivery of software source code should support activities such as compilation and debugging, and future requirements for software sustainment over the lifecycle of the program.[27]

Although notable for the recognition that software acquisition often necessarily results in the delivery of content in the form of source code, tools, databases, and the like (as opposed to hardware and physical materials), the extant guidance remains opaque in terms of the means and methods by which the government can acquire access to those deliverables. License terms—oftentimes the hallmark of contracts for delivery of a set of IP rights—receive scant attention in the instructions, which can leave PMs ill-equipped to understand the intersection of license terms, program needs, and long-term cost and effectiveness of the acquisition.

Unless and until the IP Cadre releases new guidance and instructions on how PMs and acquisition professionals should evaluate IP license terms, software-based acquisitions are likely to rely heavily on the established default Defense Federal Acquisition Regulation Supplement (DFARS) clauses in part 227.72, "Rights in Computer Software and Computer Software Documentation."[28] These contract clauses provide managers with a variety of different licenses of rights that depend on the type of IP protection that the acquired item falls under (which, in the case of software, will

---

[27] DoDI 5000.87, 2020.

[28] DoD, *Defense Federal Acquisition Regulation Supplement*, Subpart 227.72, Rights in Computer Software and Computer Software Documentation, revised March 22, 2023.

relate to technical license terms attached to the elements of the computer code). Moreover, the extent of government funding involved in the development of the code, the nature of the data (i.e., whether it is a type of data for which DoD automatically receives unlimited rights), and the agency's strategic acquisition needs will combine to provide acquisition managers flexibility under the DFARS to deliver the program what it needs via the right contracting mechanism. Nonetheless, although the DFARS provides flexibility, managers still need to know how IP concerns might intersect with program requirements to chart the most appropriate acquisition approach.

Joint Cyber Weapons' Default Licensing Terms Helped Mitigate the Lack of DoD Intellectual Property Guidance

For the JCW program, the concerns documented in the previous section are somewhat obviated by the fact that the default IP license terms on the acquired software grant "government purpose rights."[29] This set of permissions allows the government free use of the software that is consistent with the program's needs, including the granting of access to the code to government contractors as necessary for the operation and maintenance of the program. Per the terms of DFARS 227.72, government purpose rights would not allow the government to release the code publicly or to allow other third-parties to commercially sell the code, because those uses are not consistent with the program's needs.

Although JCW can operate under the standard DFARS terms, its position as a software-based acquisition program places it in the realm of programs for which further guidance, oversight, and development of DoD and Marine Corps policy is likely to emerge as the IP Cadre and its associated IP managers in the Components create and push out new IP guidance. JCW should watch the development of IP guidance carefully but the program will likely continue to be served by the extant DFARS contracting clauses.

---

[29] DoD, 2023.

The Need for IP Guidance Early in the Software Acquisition Pathway Life Cycle

Prior to the official start of the JCW acquisition program in the Software Pathway, the program was at a disadvantage because of the lack of IP guidance. IP should be considered in the early phases of acquisition, including the formulation of the contracting strategy. The JCW PM needed to determine the IP strategy well before the official SWP planning phase started because the program needed a year to complete all required contracting milestones to award a contract in time for the execution phase to start. This series of events seemed to be out of order for the typical cycle, but because of the experience that the JCW program office and contracting staff had with acquiring prior cyber operations capabilities, the difficulties had less impact than they might have for another program. Through some agility and prior experience, the JCW program office was able to work through some IP challenges; however, this might not be possible if the software program is larger or more complicated.

Information Support Plan

An ISP is a regulatory requirement for software acquisition programs entering the execution phase of the SWP per DoDI 8330.01.[30] This artifact includes a description of key aspects of the operational, systems, and technical architecture of the product being developed by the program; discusses interoperability test and certification; and serves as a key document for achieving interoperability certification. The ISP describes information technology (IT) and information needs, dependencies, and interfaces for programs in all acquisition categories. Specifically, the ISP

> is a requirement for all Information Technology (IT) programs, including National Security Systems (NSS), that connect in any way to the communications and information infrastructure. The ISP is

---

[30] DAU, "Adaptive Acquisition Framework Document Identification (AAFDID)," webpage, undated-d; DoDI 8330.01, *Interoperability of Information Technology, Including National Security Systems*, U.S. Department of Defense, September 27, 2022.

entered through the Global Information Grid Technical Guidance Federation (GTG-F) portal, and contains or links to the Net-Ready Key Performance Parameter (NR-KPP) along with supporting architectural data. Instructions for completion of the ISP are found on the GTG-F portal.[31]

The ISP focuses on the efficient and effective exchange of information that, if not properly managed, could limit or restrict the operation of the program from delivering its defined capability; it was previously known as the "C4I Support Plan." The PM uses the ISP as a tool to identify and resolve risks and issues related to a program's information through its IT infrastructure support and interface requirements. ISPs are also used to achieve CCA compliance and are a key input to a system's test plan.[32] The CCA calls for PMs to ensure that an acquisition is consistent with the DoD Information Enterprise policies and architecture, including relevant standards. This is usually done by developing a systems architecture, which is typically documented in an ISP. The NR-KPP identified in the Capability Development Document or Capability Production Document is also used in the ISP to identify support required from external information systems. Bandwidth requirement data are also documented in the ISP.

For typical programs, PMs must develop the ISP online by entering system information through the Global Information GTG-F web portal.[33] The tools on this portal do not yet support classified ISP development; classified ISPs must be completed manually in the format specified in the Defense Acquisition Guidance and GTG-F procedural documentation. Traditional ISPs contain the following types of information:

- a summary of the program's key identifying information and characteristics

---

[31] DAU, "Information Support Plan," webpage, undated-i.

[32] U.S. Code Title 40, Subtitle III: Information Technology Management.

[33] GTG-F portal can be found at: https://gtg.csd.disa.mil

- a summary description, including Operational View (OV-1) and System View (SV-1)[34]
- architectural analysis, which focuses on interoperability and supportability
  - process analysis (use cases, activity diagrams, information exchanges, etc., and additional Department of Defense Architecture Framework [DoDAF] views)
  - geospatial intelligence (GEOINT) requirements and interfaces
  - bandwidth requirements
  - NR-KPP statements (if not already in JCIDS)
  - cybersecurity survivability strategy.

We encountered the following challenges when researching and developing the ISP:

- The ISP needed to be a tailored product.
- There was inconsistency and ambiguity around commonly used terms among stakeholders.
- There was inconsistent authoritative classification of key topics and terms among stakeholders.
- There was inconsistent documentation of the core architectures involved.
- ISPs (similar to all architecture-related products) are time-intensive to develop correctly.

The ISP Needed to Be a Tailored Product

For the SWP, there has been some policy debate on the utility of ISPs (and the DoDAF) for agile software acquisition. The ISP is not directly addressed in DoDI 5000.87 but is listed under regulatory requirements in guidance that can be tailored out.[35] DIB recommended the following involving the ISP:

---

[34] U.S. Department of Defense Chief Information Officer, "The DoD Architecture Framework Version 2.02," webpage, U.S. Department of Defense, August 2010.

[35] DAU, undated-f; DoDI 5000.87, 2020.

Revise or eliminate DoDI 8330.01 to eliminate the following elements for software-intensive programs: [1] NR KPP required; [2] DoD-specific architecture products in the DoDAF format that are labor intensive and of questionable value; [e] Interoperability Support Plans (ISPs) required, where DoD [chief information officer] CIO can declare any ISP of "special interest"; [2] requirement of DT authority to provide assessments at [Milestone] MS C; [5] mandates [Joint Interoperability Test Center] JITC to do interoperability assessments for IT with "joint, multinational, and interagency interoperability requirements."[36]

The JCW program is intended to align with the JCWA and, whether it is tailored or not, the ISP is a type of operational, systems, and technical architecture reference documentation (whatever form the ISP or its replacement might take). Thus, there is a certain expected level of detail and technically authoritative information in such a reference document, and we had hoped to find some level of consistency and precision among the references we researched as we put the ISP together. Because of the uniqueness of the JCW program, subsequent challenges in trying to map a software acquisition program to traditional ISP guidance, and the evolving nature of the JCWA, the JCW program office decided to tailor the JCW ISP after coordination with the MARCORSYSCOM Chief Architect.

Specific guidance for minimum required content for the ISP and intentions for the content was drawn from DoDI 8330.01, Enclosure 3 (Procedures), Section 4.b(3) and elaborated by the JCW Product Manager.[37] Although the decision to tailor the document significantly eased the burden and level of effort for which lines of effort and types of content would be necessary to complete the ISP, there were other challenges, which we summarize in the sections that follow.

Inconsistency and Ambiguity of Key Terms

We encountered ambiguous and inconsistently applied terms across documentation of all the Service Cyber Component programs during our

---

[36] DIB, 2019b, p. S10.

[37] DoDI 8330.01, 2022.

research of the information needed to develop a tailored JCW ISP (including program names and key IT and cyber terminology). Although it was clear during our early drafts of the ISP that USCYBERCOM and its components were (slowly) working to remedy the inconsistencies by posting taxonomies and definitions of terms on its collaboration portals, the fact that terms and definitions were changing within these portals as we developed a coherent description of how JCW fits within the JCWA and its other components illustrates this point.[38]

Authoritative and consistent references for terminology are critically important for the ISP because its primary purpose is to document how the systems being developed by the affected program interconnect and interoperate with systems managed by other programs.

Inconsistent Authoritative Classification Guidance

Classification guidance for the topics and terms needed for the ISP was not available. Because ISPs frequently require a mix of information at varying levels of classification, such guidance is very helpful. A seemingly ongoing trend among Offensive Cyber Operations stakeholders to reduce previous classification levels for certain terms and topics exacerbated the lack of authoritative classification guidance. This was challenging in similar ways to the inconsistency and ambiguity of terms; we watched topics that we had previously classified at one level be reclassified at lower levels in more-recent stakeholder documents. Such documents included published architecture references.

Ensuring the correct classification at all levels is difficult when multiple stakeholders are classifying similar information in multiple ways across interrelated programs. It was clear that USCYBERCOM was taking steps to mitigate this inconsistency among its components. If such changes continue, the content of ISPs (or their replacements) will need to be periodically reviewed for such changes and any other technical details changed in the content. In our roles as derivative classifiers, our job was to do the

---

[38] Nearly all the content typical of an Offensive Cyber Operations ISP is likely to be CUI or higher, and such content is typically exchanged on high classification networks, so our descriptions here are limited to nonspecific topics and terms.

best we could with the available information and then submit the product for government review. Nevertheless, we sought to minimize work for the reviewers. Whether on the drafters' side or the reviewers' side, absence of authoritative classification guidance is at best inefficient and can at worst lead to inadvertent spillage. Providing authoritative classification guidance in a rapidly evolving, multiprogram, multicomponent acquisition effort that intends to achieve some levels of coordination and integration will continue to be a challenge.

Inconsistent Overarching and Component Architecture Documentation

During our research to pull together enough information to understand where the JCW program and its deliverables fit within USCYBERCOM's vision for JCWA, we encountered what appeared to be several generations of architecture documentation that began at JCWA's inception in 2019. Reading through these documents made clear that the vision for JCWA (the unifying architecture construct) and how each of the different component programs (including JCW) were intended to fit within JCWA had evolved and were continuing to evolve. It was a challenge to document what we considered to be the most correct description of JCW within the information in hand at the time with our knowledge that things were likely to continue to change before we even submitted our draft for review.

The real lesson learned here is already known to anyone who has attempted to apply architecture methods to rapidly evolving and agile software designs: By the time a design is understood and described, that description no longer reflects reality. The DSB certainly understands this challenge, as is reflected in its recommendations on the ISP, as does the agile community.[39] The need, then, is to figure out which type(s) and minimum level(s) of architecture documentation or content—relevant, practical, and sustainable—can coexist and serve a useful purpose within complex agile software designs that involve multiple acquisition programs coexisting, collaborating, and competing for resources and levels of effort within a common framework.

---

[39] DIB, 2019b.

Allocating Sufficient Time for Architecture Planning and Research

The three challenges that we have already discussed caused the ISP to be a time-intensive artifact to draft. Repeatedly trying to determine which term among several seemed to best apply to the same definition, which among several competing definitions of the same term was most correct, and which classification was most appropriate all required additional research, including some topics and concepts that were surprisingly fundamental to JCWA, yet ambiguous. Because we expect JCWA to continue to evolve, the lesson learned here is to allocate sufficient time for the detective work and coordination with authorities or subject-matter experts who can advise on topics that might be intentions not yet realized versus topics that are known and can be stated as facts.

For planning purposes, using the lessons learned from the challenges that we encountered, we recommend that programs track any potential reforms of the applicability of an ISP to future SWP programs, given the policy debate highlighted in the section titled "The ISP Needed to Be a Tailored Product," which appears earlier in this appendix. And, because of the multiple dependencies in information across multiple interrelated programs in an ISP, programs should also plan time to update the ISP in the execution phase.

Lifecycle Cost Estimate

Estimating the cost of investments is an important priority for DoD to ensure that investments are appropriate and affordable. According to DoD Directive 5000.01,

> MDAs [Milestone Decision Authorities] and acquisition leaders must recognize the impact of fiscal constraints and plan programs based on realistic projections of the funding available in future years.
>
> (1) To achieve affordable readiness and maintainability, MDAs and acquisition leaders, in coordination with the DoD Component programming community, will: (a) Prepare realistic program life cycle cost estimates . . . (2) The DoD Components must balance a program's require-

ments and cost in light of the funding and priorities within and across portfolios. In doing this, the DoD Component must consider both near-term development and production costs and the long-range operations and sustainment costs of deployed fleets and fielded systems.[40]

The importance of cost estimation is discussed throughout the AAF. Within the SWP, acquisition is considered up-front in the program. DoDI 5000.73 stipulates that, before the execution phase begins, the following should occur:

- The estimate should consider the technical content of the program described in the CNS, User Agreement, Acquisition Strategy, and Test Strategy.
- The initial cost estimate must be completed before entry into the execution phase and must be updated annually.
- When applicable, cost and software data reporting, including software resources data reports, must be submitted in accordance with the policies and procedures outlined in DoDI 5000.73.
- Cost estimates for programs using the embedded path of the SWP will align and integrate with the cost estimates of the weapon systems in which the software is embedded.[41]

Cost estimates in the SWP have different characteristics than cost estimates for traditional acquisitions. These differences are described in DoD's guidance for the SWP. There are some fundamental differences that require DoD's cost-estimating community to adopt different methods for estimating. For example, traditional acquisition development requires a solid cost estimate that is built on up-front analysis with small adjustments over time and coupled with regular updates at milestones; a software program requires less fidelity in the initial investment and should be refined as new information becomes available over the life of the program. Table A.1 provides a longer list of key differences between cost estimation of traditional

---

[40] DoDI 5000.01, *The Defense Acquisition System*, U.S. Department of Defense, September 9, 2020, change 1, July 28, 2022, p. 6.

[41] DoDI 5000.87, 2020, p. 15.

TABLE A.1

Key Differences Between Traditional and Agile Development Cost Estimation

	Cost Estimation for Traditional Development	Cost Estimation for Agile Development
Estimating process	Exhaustive up-front analysis with slight adjustments over time	Initial lower-fidelity baseline iteratively refined over time
Duration	Focus on life cycle as dictated by predictive program plans	Focus on near-term roadmap to inform resourcing cycle
Update timelines	Updates driven by milestones	Regular updates as new information becomes available
Team interactions	Subject-matter expert involvement up-front that is disconnected from execution	Cost analysts who are tightly coupled with subject-matter experts throughout program
Program definition	Solution defined in detail up-front with periodic updates	Near-term iterations defined with less fidelity for longer term objectives and regular updates
Cost data	Large set of program data available and solid analogous programs to reference	Emerging set of program actuals and metrics that are used to inform future iterations
Uncertainty and risk analysis	Focus on cost and schedule to meet fixed scope	Focus on variable capability given cost and schedule
Benefit analysis	No benefits realized until the end of development when software is fielded	Benefits realized more often with each fielded iteration of software

SOURCE: Adapted from DAU, "Cost Estimation," webpage, undated-e.

development versus agile acquisition. We note that operational requirements and priorities for JCW capabilities were evolving. Additionally, we applied a cost-as-an-independent-variable (CAIV) approach to estimation under uncertainty.

Agile Cost Estimation in the Face of Rapidly Emerging and Evolving Requirements

A challenging aspect of estimating the costs of agile software development projects is a lack of historical data or a detailed list of well-defined, stable requirements with distinct milestones, such as initial operational capability or full operational capability.[42] Agile development often works to a level of effort within a budget constraint, in which output is measured in terms of features or user stories delivered during each iteration or sprint. In the case of cyber weapons development, it is also common for multiple projects to be underway simultaneously, with varying levels of project size, duration, complexity and projected lifespan. Because of the need to ascertain and sustain access, some projects require more research than others, which can involve experimentation, prototyping, failure, and redirection. Over the course of product weapon development, it is not uncommon for user requirements and priorities to change before the weapon is tested and delivered. It is not a given that agile development is the best approach for all offensive cyber development, although the JCW program has adopted this development model for all its deliverables to date.

For traditional acquisition, functionality is (mostly) fixed, while time and cost are variables, and predictive cost estimation involves building the estimate from the bottom up using known or analogous estimates of work breakdown. A key challenge in estimating cost in agile offensive cyber acquisition projects is that it might not be possible to build a detailed estimate of all the development activities until a project nears completion. In agile development, the typical model is to fix time and labor and allow project scope (number of features, number of deliverables under development, delivery rate) to be variables. The bottom line is that offensive cyber weapon development needs flexible approaches to cost estimation.

Using Cost as an Independent Variable to Estimate Agile Program Costs over Time

Because of the challenges outlined previously, initial estimates for the JCW program were developed using CAIV. These estimates are generally regarded as a means of managing requirements given a cost objective.[43] In

---

[42] We use the generic term *agile development* here, but this can refer to any iterative development methods, such as DevSecOps, extreme programming, feature driven development, etc.

[43] AcqNotes, "Financial Management: Cost As an Independent Variable (CAIV)," webpage undated.

the cyber weapons example, current estimates assumed a given budget level and weapon quantities were estimated by making broad assumptions about the relative budget allocation for exploits, implants, and payloads; the time to develop the various types of weapons; the operational life of weapons; and the rate of decay of weapons' usefulness. Additional factors include cyber weapon complexity and the cost to develop and maintain weapons given the assumed complexity of the weapon.[44] Although this approach is not the standard method in the development of Program Objective Memorandum (POM) inputs, it nonetheless informs oversight on how many cyber weapons can reasonably be developed given a budget constraint.

Ideally, over time and given more historical execution data that demonstrate mission needs, the JCW program will be able to better understand cyber weapon quantity requirements and treat cost as a dependent variable, which is typically preferred in developing cost estimates for POM inputs. There are several execution metrics that would prove useful in solidifying defensible cost estimates for future POM requests. Some examples of execution data worth collecting include

- cyber weapon development duration
  - How long does it take to develop exploits, implants, and payloads?
  - What is the life cycle in cyber weapon development from researching vulnerabilities to deploying functional weapons, and are there factors that influence the duration of various steps in that life cycle?[45]
  - How does the duration of the life cycle change depending on the method of cyber weapon acquisition?[46]
- cyber weapon development cost

---

[44] For a detailed description of cost estimate assumptions, inputs, and uncertainties, see Wilson et al., 2023.

[45] Steps in the life cycle acquisition of cyber weapons might include researching potential vulnerabilities; researching options to exploit a vulnerability; the actual purchase, modification, or development of the cyber weapon; integrating and testing the weapon; deploying the weapon; and sustaining the weapon.

[46] By *method of acquisition*, we refer to whether the vulnerability or exploit is purchased, purchased and modified, or developed completely in-house.

- What resources are required to develop exploits, implants, and payloads?[47]
- How do resource requirements change for different cyber weapon acquisition methods?
- What are the resource requirements for the various life-cycle functions of a cyber weapon (e.g., research, development, integration, testing, deployment, sustainment)?
- drivers of development duration and cost
  - What are the factors or cyber weapon characteristics that influence development duration and cost?
  - This might include gathering cyber weapon characteristics, such as weapon target, exploit methodology, or other complexity factors.
- operational life of cyber weapons
  - How long is the operational life of cyber weapons?
  - What factors influence the operational life?

Product Support Strategy

Product support is a critical function performed throughout the life cycle of DoD's weapon systems and is defined by Congress as "[t]he package of support functions required to field and maintain the readiness and operational capability of covered systems, subsystems, and components, including all functions related to covered system readiness."[48] The product support activities or functions are the integrated product support elements that include

---

[47] This research could take several forms, but the number of person hours would be the most useful normalized metric. For instance, execution data might include the number of Full-Time Equivalents (FTEs) in a development scrum and the sprint duration for a given cyber weapon, which would enable the calculation of person hours for a given cyber weapon. Ideally, reporting requirements would require tracking the hours associated with each cyber weapon to avoid having to make allocation assumptions about with specific weapons.

[48] U.S. Code, Title 10, Subtitle A, Part V, Subpart F, Chapter 323, Section 4342, Life-Cycle Management and Product Support.

- product support management
- design interface
- sustaining engineering
- maintenance planning and management
- supply support
- support equipment
- technical data
- training and training support
- IT systems continuous support
- facilities and infrastructure
- packaging, handling, storage, and transportation
- manpower and personnel.[49]

DoDI 5000.91 provides further general instructions on product support planning and the development of a Product Support Strategy (PSS):

> Product support planning and PSS development begins prior to program initiation, and the resultant method of executing product support (i.e. the product support solution) is re-evaluated and updated throughout the program's life cycle. The PM, with the support of the [Product Support Manager] PSM, will begin life cycle product support planning by conducting early risk identification, mitigation, and product support analyses that inform best value solutions. The PSM must have input into systems engineering requirements, design, maintenance planning, and contract development.
>
> The PSM will collaborate with the lead systems engineer, who is responsible for executing a comprehensive reliability and maintainability program, to ensure implementation of reliability and maintainability through design, development, test, production, and sustainment. The PM and the PSM must consider total life cycle costs, schedule, per-

---

[49] Lisa P. Smith, "Product Support—The Key to Warfighter Readiness," *Defense Acquisition*, November 30, 2021. For additional details, see DAU, "DoD Integrated Product Support Implementation Roadmap," webpage, undated-g.

formance, and risks when making programmatic decisions, including decisions impacting life cycle product support.[50]

For an acquisition program in the SWP, a Product Support Strategy is required to be completed during the planning phase in order to enter the execution phase. This strategy is a regulatory requirement per DoDI 5000.87 and can be a stand-alone document or part of the Acquisition Strategy.[51] For those responsible for the Product Support Strategy, DoDI 5000.87 provides some overarching guidance as the program offices prepare documentation on this information requirement:

> (1) The PM will develop a Product Support Strategy in accordance with applicable DoDIs that treats software development as the continuing evolution of capability across the lifetime of the system, rather than assume discrete "acquisition" and "sustainment" phases. Such a strategy will incorporate early integration of key stakeholders and planning for supportability of the software from program inception, in order to facilitate software maintenance upgrades and evolution in key activities throughout the development. If using the embedded software path, the Product Support Strategy should be aligned with the overall sustainment strategy for the weapon system. The strategy should consider concurrent program activities that may span multiple funding appropriations. (2) The strategy will address contracting for tailored technical data in order to enable seamless transition of the software and its support to another organization, if and when needed. The strategy will discuss how key enabling resources (e.g., a continuous authority to operate (cATO), if applicable, automated test environments and support, a selected development environment) will transition to government or other sources of software engineering competence. The strategy will include how any transitions allow for continuous testing and monitoring, and address the need to provide subject matter experts

---

[50] DoDI 5000.91, *Product Support Management for the Adaptive Acquisition Framework*, U.S. Department of Defense, November 4, 2021, p. 12.

[51] DAU, "Execution Phase," webpage, undated-h.

and/or ensure all software engineering staff are trained in the tools, techniques, and environments.[52]

During our research for development of the Product Support Strategy, we used a section of the JCW Acquisition Strategy as a template for the Product Support Strategy. Additionally, the Product Support Strategy needed to be tailored to the characteristics of the JCW program.

The Product Support Section of the Joint Cyber Weapon Acquisition Strategy Served as the Template

The JCW program office was asked to address product support during the planning phase for the JCW program. In the absence of a stand-alone template for Product Support Strategies in the SWP, the guidance from the Acquisition Strategy section on product support was used to inform the structure and types of information needed for the JCW Product Support Strategy.

Using the Acquisition Strategy guidance, other product support guidance, and a significant level of tailoring, this strategy ultimately covered

- roles and responsibilities
- development to support transition
- weapon repositories
- service-level agreements
- maintenance of relevancy
- readiness testing
- maintenance
- reuse and redeployment
- hardware and software tools to support the program.

Discussions were held with the user community to determine roles and responsibilities of both the JCW program office and user community. There were also discussions with the JCW program office about how the contractor and test communities would be involved during the life cycle of the JCW

---

[52] DoDI 5000.87, 2020, p. 15.

capabilities. The technical approach was an important source of information for this artifact.

The Product Support Strategy Was a Tailored Product

Given the uniqueness of this cyber operations program, the Product Support Strategy was tailored to a variety of factors, including that, once delivered, the solutions would not be modified. However, there were updates as developers continued to work on solutions (in many cases, for other customers) that could be used to update JCW solutions. There is also the potential or need for updates to a product because of performance. Some products might not be available for further use, but others can be retained for lesser capable targets.

Although some of the artifacts for the JCW program will need to be modified, the Product Support Strategy might not need as many revisions during the execution phase because the JCW program is not fielding a weapon system with a decades-long life cycle.

Test Strategy

Acquisition programs are required to go through testing before the capability is provided to the warfighter. Programs are typically tested in both developmental and operational environments before being fielded. DAU's SWP site refers to testing throughout its guidance sections for a variety of reasons, which illustrates the importance of testing to programs in the SWP.[53] A Test Strategy is a regulatory requirement for entrance into the execution phase.[54] The Test Strategy might be part of Acquisition Strategy, or some program on the Director, Operational Test and Evaluation Oversight list might require a more detailed Test and Evaluation Master Plan.

Conducting iterative testing is a key part of modern software practices. According to OSD guidance:

---

[53] DoDI 5000.87, 2020.

[54] DAU, undated-d.

The software pathway focuses on modern iterative software development techniques such as agile, lean, and development security operations, which promise faster delivery of working code to the user. The goal of this software acquisition pathway is to achieve continuous integration and continuous delivery to the maximum extent possible. Integrated testing, to include contractor testing, is a critical component needed to reach this goal. Identifying integrated T&E and interoperability requirements early in Test Strategy development will enable streamlined integration, developmental and operational T&E, interoperability certification, and faster delivery to the field. The program Acquisition Strategy must clearly identify T&E requirements that have been fully coordinated with the test community.[55]

The Test Strategy for programs in the SWP should include

- an approach to developing measurable criteria derived from requirements (e.g., user features, user stories, use cases)
- identification of test platforms and infrastructure (automated testing and plans for accreditation) and T&E costs
- a description of what the contractor will provide and on what schedule
- methods for streamlining testing
- system-level and nonfunctional performance requirements
- independent organizations with roles, responsibilities, and established agreements
- identification of any safety critical risks, along with an approach to manage them
- plans for automated data collection for use in value assessments
- plans for integrating developmental and operational test when possible
- discussion on how cybersecurity developmental and operational T&E assessments are integrated into the overall test plans.[56]

During our development of the JCW Test Strategy, we were able to follow the SWP Test Strategy template for structure and content. We also needed

---

[55] DAU, "Test Strategy," webpage, undated-o.

[56] DAU, undated-o; DoDI 5000.89, *Test and Evaluation*, U.S. Department of Defense, November 19, 2020.

to account for JCW's contract developers and other JCWA stakeholders in the Test Strategy.

The Published Test Strategy Template Was Sufficient for Joint Cyber Weapons' Test Strategy

OSD created a Test Strategy template specifically for the SWP.[57] The JCW program office largely followed the topics in the template with some minor tailoring. Within this plan, the uniqueness of the JCW program created some challenges. For example, the variety of products produced (e.g., implants, exploits, payloads) made it difficult to tailor a single overall Test Strategy for the program. In addition, another unique aspect of the JCW program is that testing needs to happen in an isolated environment that mirrors the operational environment; products can never be fully tested until they are operationalized in the field.[58]

The Test Strategy Might Involve Coordination with External Stakeholders

Because the JCW program sits among various program components of the JCWA and because of USCYBERCOM's vision and intentions for the JCWA, much of JCW's individual test plan content depends on external JCW contract developers and other stakeholders. In this case, there is a division of testing responsibilities among external contractors, the JCW program, and the USCYBERCOM sponsor where the lines of responsibilities were difficult to clearly delineate and seem to be evolving. We expect such arrangements are likely to be common for other software acquisition programs and should be addressed in guidance. Finally, because of the evolving nature of the affected programs or architectures, the resulting testing process might be fluid as well, which means that the Test Strategy will likely need to be updated periodically in the execution phase.

---

[57] DAU, "SWP Artifact Templates," webpage, undated-n.

[58] In other words, fully testing a cyber weapon requires the existence or cooperation of one or more adversary vulnerabilities as part of the end-to-end execution of the intended effect.

User Agreement

Section 872 of the FY18 NDAA directed the DIB to undertake its study on streamlining software development and acquisition regulations. As part of its findings, the DIB recommended that

> DoD should manage software by measuring value delivered to the user rather than by monitoring compliance with requirements. Accountability should be based on delivering value to the user and solving user needs, not on complying with obsolete contracts or requirements documents.[59]

Understanding what value means to the user requires discussions with the user community of a weapon system throughout the software acquisition life cycle. As a result of this and other recommendations for best practices in modern software acquisition, a formal User Agreement is a regulatory requirement that must be drafted during the planning phase in preparation for the execution phase of the SWP.[60]

OSD provides additional guidance to both the acquisition and user communities as programs are preparing for the SWP. Some of the key tenets for user participation during the acquisition life cycle are as follows:

> Agile software methodologies require users to make a commitment to the program to enable successful execution. Effective software acquisition requires engagement with users to understand their concepts of operations, environment, existing capabilities, external systems with which the required capability must interface, interoperability requirements, threats, and other specific needs. This may require additional and/or separate funding to ensure users have the resources to support as needed.[61]

Following our research and development of the User Agreement, it is worth noting that the newness of the guidance for User Agreements in the

---

[59] DIB, 2019a, p. 7.

[60] DAU, undated-d; DoDI 5000.87, 2020, p. 10.

[61] DAU, undated-c.

SWP meant that the SWP-provided template could be followed with little tailoring and that developing the User Agreement was beneficial to both users and the program office. Additionally, the lengthy development process for the User Agreement and its concurrency with other SWP artifacts required many revisions and additional vetting.

The Published User Agreement Template Was Sufficient with Little Tailoring

The JCW program office initiated the work on the User Agreement using the User Agreement template on DAU's website.[62] Because the User Agreement was a newer information requirement in both communities, there was minimal tailoring of the User Agreement template by the JCW program office and the user community. Following OSD's guidance closely, the JCW program User Agreement

- defines roles and responsibilities along with specific commitments by the sponsor, project or product team, and user communities
- establishes how the JCW program will address user priority needs and support active collaboration among the operational users, acquisition community, and software development teams
- ensures that the sponsor, users, and stakeholder inputs are integrated into value assessments.

The following specific actions are also included in regard to additional information defined in OSD's guidance for a User Agreement:

- planning anticipated developer and user ceremonies, events, and interactions
- prioritizing features and stories in roadmaps and backlogs against the overarching CNS
- determining MVP, MVCR, and other releases
- developing and participating in user training and knowledge sharing
- performing user testing and software demonstrations

---

[62] DAU, undated-n.

- making decisions regarding software release and deployment.[63]

Development of the User Agreement Benefited the User Community and the Joint Cyber Weapon Project Management Office

Developing the JCW User Agreement required agreement between the acquisition and user communities on many touchpoints that, previously, would not have been formally defined or even discussed unless needed. The two communities established a closer working relationship through these discussions, which should ultimately benefit the stakeholders going forward. In addition, many parts of the User Agreement were then applicable to other documentation being drafted for the program. These were critical inputs for several of the artifacts, including the Acquisition Strategy, Product Support, and Test Strategy.

Concurrency with Other Artifacts and Time Needed for Vetting Were Challenging

Despite the benefits described in previous sections, there were challenges in drafting the User Agreement. For example, it took a long time to draft the document and to achieve agreement among multiple stakeholders from different organizations. It was one of the last documents to be formally approved, but it still needed to be drafted such that pieces of the document could be used in other SWP artifacts. The concurrency of drafting this document and others required many revisions and additional quality assurance because of potential errors in consistency among multiple moving pieces.

Some additional, more nuanced lessons learned were discovered during the process of drafting the User Agreement, including the following:

- Clear delineation between *developmental* T&E and *operational* T&E needs to be established, in addition to who performs what for software programs. This delineation would affect not only the User Agreement

---

[63] DAU, undated-c.

and Project Support Strategy but also the Test Strategy and the Acquisition Strategy.

- There might not be enough personnel qualified or available to be tool champions.[64] As a result, steps that should be conducted independently in the developmental T&E and operational T&E steps can potentially be conducted by the same person, thus missing the required independent review. The shortage also creates a potential choke point for multiple JCWs being developed that all rely on the same one or two individuals.
- A definition of *Lead User Representative* and that individual's authorities should be codified by the Marine Corps. It can be assumed that the Lead User Representative is also a User, but not any User can be the Lead User Representative with the authority to develop and validate CNS(s) and Capability Needs Forms or assign users to work each Capability Needs Forms.

Because a formal User Agreement is a new artifact in software acquisition, there should be careful review during the execution phase of the JCW program to ensure that both communities are able to provide the benefits envisioned by this artifact. Revisions might need to happen if new concerns or challenges arise within either community, particularly as the Value Assessments are being conducted, which will provide the opportunity for the user community to determine value and adjust practices within the program office to achieve that value.

---

[64] *Tool champions* are the designated experts and advocates for specific types of cyber tools who are counted on for independent code reviews and developmental and operational testing.

Abbreviations

AAF	Adaptive Acquisition Framework
CAIV	cost as an independent variable
CCA	Clinger Cohen Act
CNS	Capability Needs Statement
DAU	Defense Acquisition University
DA	Decision Authority
DevSecOps	development, security, and operations
DFARS	Defense Federal Acquisition Regulation Supplement
DIB	Defense Innovation Board
DoD	U.S. Department of Defense
DoDAF	Department of Defense Architecture Framework
DoDI	Department of Defense Instruction
DSB	Defense Science Board
FY	fiscal year
GAO	U.S. Government Accountability Office
GTG-F	Grid Technical Guidance Federation
IP	intellectual property
ISP	Information Support Plan
IT	information technology
JCIDS	Joint Capabilities Integration and Development System
JCW	Joint Cyber Weapons
JCWA	Joint Cyber Warfighting Architecture
MARCORSYSCOM	Marine Corps Systems Command
MVCR	minimum viable capability release
MVP	minimum viable product
NDAA	National Defense Authorization Act

NR-KPP	Net-Ready Key Performance Parameter
OSD	Office of the Secretary of Defense
PMO	Program Management Office
PM	Program Manager
POM	Program Objective Memorandum
PSM	Product Support Manager
SECNAVINST	Secretary of the Navy Instruction
SWP	Software Acquisition Pathway
T&E	test and evaluation
USCYBERCOM	U.S. Cyber Command

References

Ablon, Lillian, and Andy Bogart, *Zero Days, Thousands of Nights: The Life and Times of Zero-Day Vulnerabilities and Their Exploits*, RAND Corporation, RR-1751-RC, 2017. As of June 23, 2023:
https://www.rand.org/pubs/research_reports/RR1751.html

AcqNotes, "Financial Management: Cost as an Independent Variable (CAIV)," webpage, undated. As of June 23, 2023:
https://acqnotes.com/acqnote/careerfields/cost-as-an-independent-variable

Agile Alliance, homepage, undated. As of June 23, 2023:
https://www.agilealliance.org

Bellovin, Steven M., Susan Landau, and Herbert S. Lin, "Limiting the Undesired Impact of Cyber Weapons: Technical Requirements and Policy Implications," *Journal of Cybersecurity*, Vol. 3, No. 1, March 2017.

Brady, Sean, "DoD's Software Acquisition Pathway, Digital Delivery at the Speed of Relevance," DAU West—Let's Talk Agile briefing, January 6, 2020.

Brady, Sean, "DoD's Software Acquisition Pathway: Digital Delivery at the Speed of Relevance, First Annual State of the SWP," Let's Talk Agile Series briefing, October 6, 2021.

Brady, Sean, "Adaptive Acquisition Framework (AAF) Vignette Middle Tier of Acquisition (MTA) and Software Acquisition Pathway (SWP) Hybrid," Defense Acquisition University, July 2022a.

Brady, Sean, "DoD's Software Acquisition Pathway, Digital Delivery at the Speed of Relevance," DAU—Let's Talk Agile briefing, July 27, 2022b.

CAPEC—*See* Common Attack Pattern Enumeration and Classification.

Common Attack Pattern Enumeration and Classification, "CAPEC Glossary," webpage, MITRE Corporation, undated. As of June 23, 2023:
https://capec.mitre.org/about/glossary.html

DAU—*See* Defense Acquisition University.

Defense Acquisition University, "Acquisition Guidebooks & References," webpage, undated-a. As of June 23, 2023:
https://aaf.dau.edu/guidebooks/

Defense Acquisition University, "Acquisition Strategy," webpage, undated-b. As of June 23, 2023:
https://aaf.dau.edu/aaf/software/acquisition-strategy/

Defense Acquisition University, "Active User Engagement," webpage, undated-c. As of June 23, 2023:
https://aaf.dau.edu/aaf/software/active-user-engagement/

Defense Acquisition University, "Adaptive Acquisition Framework Document Identification (AAFDID)," webpage, undated-d. As of June 23, 2023:
https://www.dau.edu/aafdid/Pages/
SWA-Application-and-Embedded-SW-Information-Requirements.aspx

Defense Acquisition University, "Cost Estimation," webpage, undated-e. As of June 23, 2023:
https://aaf.dau.edu/aaf/software/cost-estimation/

Defense Acquisition University, "Develop Strategies," webpage, undated-f. As of June 23, 2023:
https://aaf.dau.edu/aaf/software/develop-strategies/

Defense Acquisition University, "DoD Integrated Product Support Implementation Roadmap," webpage, undated-g. As of June 23, 2023:
https://www.dau.edu/dodpsroadmap/Pages/Default.aspx

Defense Acquisition University, "Execution Phase," webpage, undated-h. As of June 23, 2023:
https://aaf.dau.edu/aaf/software/execution-phase/

Defense Acquisition University, "Information Support Plan," webpage, undated-i. As of June 23, 2023:
https://www.dau.edu/glossary/Pages/Glossary.aspx#!both|I|27659

Defense Acquisition University, "Program Management Metrics and Reporting," webpage, undated-j. As of June 23, 2023:
https://aaf.dau.edu/aaf/software/metrics-and-reporting/

Defense Acquisition University, "Software Acquisition," webpage, undated-k. As of June 23, 2023:
https://aaf.dau.edu/aaf/software/

Defense Acquisition University, *Software Acquisition Pathway Quick Start Primer*, undated-l.

Defense Acquisition University, "Software in NDAAs," webpage, undated-m. As of June 23, 2023:
https://aaf.dau.edu/aaf/software/ndaa/

Defense Acquisition University, "SWP Artifact Templates," webpage, undated-n. As of June 23, 2023:
https://aaf.dau.edu/aaf/software/templates/

Defense Acquisition University, "Test Strategy," webpage, undated-o. As of June 23, 2023:
https://aaf.dau.edu/aaf/software/test-strategy/

Defense Innovation Board, "Who Cares: Why Does Software Matter for DoD?" in *Software Acquisition and Practices (SWAP) Study Main Report*, U.S. Department of Defense, May 2019a.

Defense Innovation Board, *Software Is Never Done: Refactoring the Acquisition Code for Competitive Advantage*, U.S. Department of Defense, May 3, 2019b.

Defense Science Board, *Design and Acquisition of Software for Defense Systems*, Department of Defense, February 2018.

Defense Technical Information Center, "Section 809 Panel," webpage, undated. As of June 23, 2023:
https://discover.dtic.mil/section-809-panel/

Department of Defense Directive 5000.01, *The Defense Acquisition System*, U.S. Department of Defense, September 9, 2020, change 1, July 28, 2022.

Department of Defense Instruction 5000.02, *Operation of the Adaptive Acquisition Framework*, U.S. Department of Defense, January 23, 2020.

Department of Defense Instruction 5000.87, *Operation of the Software Acquisition Pathway*, U.S. Department of Defense, October 2, 2020.

Department of Defense Instruction 5000.89, *Test and Evaluation*, U.S. Department of Defense, November 19, 2020.

Department of Defense Instruction 5000.91, *Product Support Management for the Adaptive Acquisition Framework*, U.S. Department of Defense, November 4, 2021.

Department of Defense Instruction 5010.44, *Intellectual Property (IP) Acquisition and Licensing*, U.S. Department of Defense, October 16, 2019.

Department of Defense Instruction 8330.01, *Interoperability of Information Technology, Including National Security Systems*, U.S. Department of Defense, September 27, 2022.

Department of Defense Standard Practice MIL-STD-881F, *Work Breakdown Structures for Defense Material Items*, U.S. Department of Defense, May 13, 2022.

DIB—*See* Defense Innovation Board.

DoDI—*See* Department of Defense Instruction.

GAO—*See* US. Government Accountability Office.

Gartner, "Information Technology Gartner Glossary," webpage, undated. As of June 23, 2023:
https://www.gartner.com/en/chat/information-technology/glossary

Gartner Peer Insights, homepage, undated. As of June 23, 2023:
https://www.gartner.com/peer-insights/home

Manifesto for Agile Software Development, homepage, undated. As of June 23, 2023:
https://agilemanifesto.org

McKernan, Megan, Jeffrey A. Drezner, and Jerry M. Sollinger, *Tailoring the Acquisition Process in the U.S. Department of Defense*, RAND Corporation, RR-966-OSD, 2015. As of June 23, 2023:
https://www.rand.org/pubs/research_reports/RR966.html

Public Law 114-92, National Defense Authorization Act for Fiscal Year 2016, November 25, 2015.

Public Law 115–91, National Defense Authorization Act for Fiscal Year 2018, December 12, 2017.

Public Law 116-92, National Defense Authorization Act for Fiscal Year 2020, December 20, 2019.

Public Law 116-283, William M. (Mac) Thornberry National Defense Authorization Act for Fiscal Year 2021, November 27, 2019.

SECNAVINST—*See* Secretary of the Navy Instruction.

Secretary of the Navy Instruction 5000.2G, *Department of the Navy Implementation of the Defense Acquisition System and the Adaptive Acquisition Framework*, Office of the Secretary, Department of the Navy , April 8, 2022.

Smith, Lisa P., "Product Support—The Key to Warfighter Readiness," *Defense Acquisition*, November 30, 2021.

U.S. Code, Title 10, Subtitle A, Part V, Subpart F, Chapter 322, Subchapter 1, Section 4211, Acquisition Strategy.

U.S. Code Title 10, Subtitle A, Part V, Subpart F, Chapter 323, Section 4342, Life-Cycle Management and Product Support.

U.S. Code Title 40, Subtitle III: Information Technology Management.

U.S. Department of Defense, *DoD Enterprise DevSecOps Reference Design*, version 1.0, August 12, 2019.

U.S. Department of Defense, *Cybersecurity Strategy Outline and Guidance*, June 24, 2021a.

U.S. Department of Defense, *Department of Defense Software Modernization Strategy*, version 1.0, November 2021b.

U.S. Department of Defense, *Defense Federal Acquisition Regulation Supplement*, Subpart 227.72, Rights in Computer Software and Computer Software Documentation, revised March 22, 2023.

U.S. Department of Defense Chief Information Officer, "The DoD Architecture Framework Version 2.02," webpage, U.S. Department of Defense, August 2010. As of June 23, 2023:
https://dodcio.defense.gov/library/dod-architecture-framework/

U.S. Government Accountability Office, *Defense Acquisitions: Major Weapon Systems Continue to Experience Cost and Schedule Problems under DoD's Revised Policy*, April 13, 2006.

U.S. Government Accountability Office, *DoD Space Acquisitions: Including Users Early and Often in Software Development Could Benefit Programs*, March 18, 2019.

U.S. Government Accountability Office, *Software Development: DoD Faces Risks and Challenges in Implementing Modern Approaches and Addressing Cybersecurity Practices*, June 23, 2021a.

U.S. Government Accountability Office, *Defense Acquisitions: DoD Should Take Additional Actions to Improve How it Approaches Intellectual Property*, November 30, 2021b.

U.S. Government Accountability Office, *Leading Practices: Agency Acquisition Policies Could Better Implement Key Product Development Principles*, March 10, 2022.

U.S. Marine Corps Systems Command, *Decision Memorandum for Joint Cyber Weapons: Payloads, Exploits, and Implants Program Use of the Software Acquisition Pathway and Entry into the Planning Phase*, October 22, 2021, Not available to the general public.

Wilson, Bradley, Thomas Goughnour, Megan McKernan, Andrew Karode, Devin Tierney, Mark V. Arena, Michael J. D. Vermeer, Hansell Perez, and Alexis Levedahl, *A Cost Estimating Framework for U.S. Marine Corps Joint Cyber Weapons*, RAND Corporation, RR-A1124-1, 2023. As of June 23, 2023:
https://www.rand.org/pubs/research_reports/RRA1124-1.html

Wong, Jonathan P., Obaid Younossi, Christine Kistler LaCoste, Philip S. Anton, Alan J. Vick, Guy Weichenberg, and Thomas C. Whitmore, *Improving Defense Acquisition: Insights from Three Decades of RAND Research*, RAND Corporation, RR-A1670-1, 2022. As of June 23, 2023:
https://www.rand.org/pubs/research_reports/RRA1670-1.html